The Romany Good Spell Book

Gillian Kemp is a freelance writer and astrologer who first encountered Romanies while growing up in rural Hertfordshire and Bedfordshire. As a journalist she met Olive Cox, the last Romany girl in this country to be born, marry and bear her own children in a horse-drawn caravan.

Her horoscope columns appear regularly in *Baby* and *Your Health* magazines, and she is a frequent contributor to cable television. Her work as a clairvoyant has brought her into contact with numerous celebrities to whom she has given readings.

Gillian Kemp lives in Buckinghamshire with her beloved dog, Daisy May.

The Romany
Good Spell Book

GILLIAN KEMP

VISTA

First published in Great Britain 1997
as a Vista paperback original

Vista is an imprint of the Cassell Group
Wellington House, 125 Strand, London WC2R 0BB

A catalogue record for this book is
available from the British Library.

ISBN 0 575 60244 9

Typeset in Great Britain by
Rowland Phototypesetting Ltd
Bury St Edmunds, Suffolk
Printed in Great Britain by
Cox & Wyman Ltd, Reading, Berkshire

To my father Mike; mother Ruth, in spirit;
sisters Lynette and Alison; brother Nigel;
my faithful Yorkshire terrier, Daisy May,
and her godmother, Katie Boyle.

To my agent Chelsey, publisher Faith and to
the one I love.

Thank you also to Peter Ingram
of the Romany Folklore Museum.

Contents

The Romany Trail   9

Romany Sorcery   17

Spells   25

    Love   29

    Health   79

    Pets   105

    Wealth   113

    Happiness   133

The Romany Trail

On the eve of the twenty-first century the ancient world seems as distant as an old man's recollection of childhood. The Aztecs, the Chaldeans, Homer's Greece, the England of King Arthur, and Avalon have long since vanished. Only the Romanies, miraculously, survive, providing us with a flesh and blood link with the roots of civilization.

Like much that was extraordinary, this tribe of nomads emerged from the East, first setting foot in Europe nine centuries ago. At once, they became objects of wonder, hatred and controversy, and were to remain so. Christian bishops deplored them. They were enslaved, hunted down, and deprived of civil rights. Hitler was to persecute them as relentlessly as he tormented the Jews.

In the British Isles, society remains puzzled by the wanderers in its midst. Are they really a unique race of healers and clairvoyants? Or are they charlatans and parasites?

Whatever the case, the Romanies remain apart from the rest of us, indifferent to our electronic culture and clinging as best they can to age-old customs, courtship rights and dialect.

So who are they and where do they really come from? The Romany language provides us with a clue. It contains elements of Kashmiri, Hindi, Gujarati, Marathi, Nepali and Urdu. Some words are derived from Sanskrit, the oldest and most sacred language in the Indian subcontinent. A Romany could converse quite fluently with sections of our Asian community.

But Romanes is an oral language. Every Romany is a skilful storyteller. Romany lore is passed from generation to generation by word of mouth. Smart and Crofton compiled a *Dictionary of the English Gypsies* in 1874, and in the same year, George Borrow assembled a dictionary called *Romano Lavo Lil* which means 'gypsy word book'. Later, in 1926, Dr John Sampson published the dialect of the gypsies of Wales, which is the older form of Romanes. But the Romanies themselves have not written any books at all until fairly modern times.

The first Romanies pursued the precarious life of farmers in the inhospitable Hindu Kush region of Kashmir and Afghanistan. They were known to neighbouring tribes as Jat, Zott, Luli, Nuri or Dom. Here they would have become steeped in the timeless wisdom of the Orient. No one is certain what prompted the astonishing migration that was to take them halfway across the world.

They headed first for what is now Iran, where in the tenth century AD Hamsa of Isfahan logged the arrival of 12,000 gaudy musicians. The nomads dallied long enough to absorb some Persian dialects into their own language before moving on. Some drifted west while others journeyed north into Armenia and the Caucasus. By the twelfth century they were exploring Greece. In 1322, two friars on their way to the Holy Land, Simon Simeonis and Hugh the Enlightened, described an encounter with a tribe of exotic nomads in Crete who slept in tents and caves. They were noted fortune-tellers and musicians.

One community of Romanies founded a Balkan ghetto known as 'Little Egypt' where they built huts and prospered as metal smiths. The tribal elders were known as the Dukes or Counts of Little Egypt. It was here that the strangers from the East first became known as Egyptians, Gitans or Gypsies.

Illiterate the Romanies may have been, and inclined to pagan practices such as fortune-telling, but they were shrewd enough to court favour with the Church once they had entered Christian Europe. For instance they discovered that the most privileged travellers of the day were Christian pilgrims, and mingled with them. By the time they reached Europe in 1427, they had acquired letters of recognition from imposing figures such as the Emperor Sigismund of Poland.

In Italy, Duke Andre and his picturesque companions mollified pious onlookers by asserting that they were on their way to see the Pope. No account of any such audience is to be found in the Vatican archives. But there is reason to believe that their representatives did meet Pope Martin V (1417–31), who is said to have imposed a penance. This was that they should 'roam the earth for seven years without sleeping in a bed'. He then sent them on their way with a papal blessing. Soon afterwards, thousands pitched their tents at the gates of Paris.

Contemporary chroniclers were impressed by the spectacle. One noted that 'Their children were incredibly shrewd and the majority, indeed nearly all of them, had their ears pierced and in each, wore one or two silver rings.' Another reporter remarked that 'The men were very dark and their hair was crisp.' He was less kind in his description of the women, who were, he said, the 'ugliest and swarthiest one could see'. Some of them were even tattooed!

He noted that 'There were among them witches who looked at people's hands, revealed the past and foretold the future.' This talent was to prove dangerous for unfaithful wives and husbands. And for many of the gypsy seers it was to prove fatal. They were tried for sorcery or on trumped-up charges of theft and deception. Gallows were erected. On one of these, at the Porte Saint-Denis, the victims included a hurdy-gurdy man and his wife. This public execution attracted an enormous crowd: 'especially women and girls, for it was a great novelty to see a woman hanged in France', said an observer at the time.

Happier days awaited them in Spain, where Count Miguel Lucas De Iranzo the Constable of Castile invited them into his castle at Jaen and welcomed them as magicians and entertainers.

Restless as ever, some of the adventurers embarked for the British Isles, where they aroused more excitement and curiosity. It is highly probable that gypsies were in Britain well before the documented account of their arrival by the Lord High Treasurer of Scotland in 1505.

For a while all went well. King James IV of Scotland commended them to the King of Denmark. In 1519, the Earl of Surrey entertained a party of them at his Suffolk home. Town dwellers were fascinated by the Romany arts of palmistry and second sight, but country people resented the newcomers, whom they accused of stealing their cattle and abducting their children.

The Romanies were savagely purged by Henry VIII, while Elizabeth I blamed them for treacherous liaisons with papist conspirators. In 1563 she ordered all gypsies to leave the country within three months or suffer arrest and execution. Five men were hanged in Durham 'for being Egyptians'. The Romanies fell out of favour north of the border as well: four were hanged in Edinburgh in 1611 'for abyding within the kingdome they being Egiptienis'.

There were fearful pogroms in Europe. In Spain, a Romany could be shot on sight. Although murderers and rapists could seek sanctuary in church, this remarkable privilege was denied to Romanies. Their very existence was regarded as criminal. There were no safe havens. If they were lucky they were transported. The less fortunate had their ears chopped off.

In Romania entire families could be bought and sold. This practice continued until the middle of the nineteenth century. Sales were advertised in Bucharest newspapers.

In the United Kingdom the canniest Romanies saved themselves from further trouble by adopting safe and familiar names, such as Smith and Boswell. They merged with the native population and earned a living and grudging respect as tinsmiths, coppersmiths and blacksmiths.

But the suffering of the Romanies was by no means over. Half a million are feared to have perished in Auschwitz and other Nazi extermination factories. Their fate had been sealed by the Nazis in the Nuremberg decree of 15 September 1935, which was 'unanimously adopted' by the German parliament, the Reichstag. The decree was aimed primarily at depriving Jews of German citizenship. One of its authors, Dr Hans Globke, said that he also regarded gypsies as being of 'alien blood'. At that time, Eva Justin of the Reich Race Research Division added to their woe by declaring that 'Gypsy blood was very dangerous for the purity of the German race'.

A decree of 14 December 1937 described them as 'inveterate criminals'. Thousands of Romany men, women and children were herded into camps. The women became victims of hideous medical experiments at Ravensbrück, where SS doctors advocated mass sterilization of the nomads.

After the outbreak of war in 1939, they found themselves in peril in every country occupied by the German armies. But not even the Nazis could eliminate this race of survivors. Romany communities are still to be found the length and breadth of Europe and deep inside the former Soviet Union. The family of wanderers is smaller than before, less conspicuous and as watchful as always. Most continue to be ostracized and tolerated rather than cherished.

But the Romanies have not only survived; they have preserved their integrity. In a chaotic era in which family life appears to be disintegrating, the Romanies remain men and women of strict principle. In their daily attitudes to courtship, marriage, children, the care of animals and personal hygiene they can be correct to the point of prissiness.

Not for nothing are the Romanies known as 'The Last Victorians'. It was during the reign of Queen Victoria that the wanderers adopted the horse-drawn wagon or *vardo*. They finally discarded the tents which had provided them with shelter during their long and eventful odyssey from Asia.

Painstakingly embellished with gold leaf and ornately furnished with a fireplace, mahogany panelling and cut glass mirrors, these Victorian mobile homes resembling Renaissance palaces were warmer, cosier and more welcoming than cottages. They were to inspire countless paintings, poems, romantic novels and children's stories.

Like the Romany campfires around which the musical travellers sang and danced, the wagons promised companionship, freedom and good cheer. But in Britain today, barely a dozen families are to be found wandering the country in horse-drawn wagons.

In a decade or so there may be none at all. If so, rural life will be much the poorer, for Romanies are true friends of the earth. With their nomadic existence they have lived closer to nature for longer than anyone else. No one respects the environment more. They are among the last free spirits on the face of the globe.

Romany Sorcery

Early man was hunched. His eyes were downcast. His first sight of the heavens would have been the puzzling reflections of the sun, the moon and the stars in lakes and running water.

Later he looked upwards and marvelled at their mirror image. It was now that the concepts of gods, creation and mortality evolved, and with it the human wish to make sense of the infinite and to gaze into the future. All the ancient cultures were psychic cultures.

Divination in one form or another was practised by the ancient Greeks, Chinese, Incas, Mayans, Arabs, Egyptians, Hindus, Chaldeans, Polynesians and the Australian Aborigines. Some of them detected visions in liquid. This was known as hydromancy, water being the first medium employed. The Greeks meditated at sacred pools. The Egyptians scrutinized blobs of ink, the Hindus consulted bowls of molasses, while others read messages in clouds. Many gazed into fragments of crystal or precious stones. The Romanies, themselves an ancient race from the East, were enthusiastic and gifted practitioners of divination.

The first card players are believed to have been the

Chinese. But it was the Tarot that most fascinated the Europeans, much to the disgust of the Church, which mistrusted fortune telling and still does.

Tarot cards are believed to be derived from the *Book of Thoth*. Thoth was revered as an ancient Egyptian 'scribe of the Gods' and was patron of sacred wisdom, learning and literature. The Romanies adopted the Tarot and claim to have introduced it to Europe on their arrival in 1427. This is debatable, but what is sure is that the Romanies helped to spread its use.

Cards of all sorts were condemned: in England, Henry VIII tried to suppress them. Tarot cards were abolished during his reign, which is why today's playing cards feature, unchanged throughout history, the Royal Court fashion of his era.

In 1526 the Reverend John Northbrooke of Bristol devoted a passionate sermon to the topic of playing cards which he regarded as 'an invention of the Devil'. He would have been even more disquieted by Tarot cards, since they had been inspired by a heathen god of magic whom the Pharaohs had worshipped in Old Testament Eygpt. (A 'heathen' was probably someone who lived on the heath.)

The Romanies were also enthusiasts in palmistry, the age-old art of divining strangers' past and probable fate from the lines on their hands. The practice is said to have been widespread in China as early as 3000 BC. Aristotle and Pliny the Elder were among the prominent ancients who believed in palmistry, but it was not until the fifteenth century that it became established in Western Europe.

The popularity of palmistry coincided with the Romany trek through Germany, France and Spain to the British Isles. In those days it was believed that the hand was considered in relation to the complete physical and spiritual nature of a person and hand reading involved strong moral judgments and prophecies of fate no matter how calamitous.

Even in an age as agnostic as our own, there are those who consult their palmist before making decisions or deciding on a course of action. Many of these palmists are of Romany blood.

Palmistry enjoyed the blessing of the Swiss psychologist, Dr Carl Jung. In the introduction to Julius Spier's *The Hands of Children* he concluded that 'the totality conception of modern biology, which is based on the evidence of a host of observations and research, does not exclude the possibility that hands whose shape and functioning are so intimately connected with the psyche, might provide revealing and therefore interpretable expressions of psychical peculiarity, that is, of the human character'.

The human hand, palmists insist, is a map of life and can be read as fluently as the human face. Even though they were at one time accused of witchcraft, palmists have never claimed occult powers. They regard palmistry as a craft. In Romany families, girls as young as six are taught palmistry just as other children are introduced to the alphabet.

At least as old as palmistry is faith in the power of crystals. The first seers relied on pieces of ice. The word 'crystal' is Greek in origin and means 'clear ice' or 'frozen water'. At the time of Christ, sorcerers claimed astonishing powers for crystals: it was said they could reveal the course of history and the fate of rulers.

Learned men such as the Roman philosopher, Seneca, believed in them, although the pagan priests of those days were notorious for their cynicism.

The first crystal balls, spheres of rock crystal, onyx or volcanic glass, in Britain appeared in the fifteenth century. The seers often assumed a trance-like state as they interpreted the contents of the globe. Sometimes they saw, or thought they saw, symbols that were of heavenly origin. Sometimes they were confronted by images of momentous events.

Monarchs such as Elizabeth I, a woman normally noted as being down to earth and who despised humbug, were intrigued. Certainly she enjoyed the presence at her Court of the astrologer, Dr John Dee. He described his crystal ball as his 'Shew-stone', and swore that an angel had given it to him.

Less extravagant claims are made by the present generation of crystal ball gazers!

The art is also less expensive than it was at the time of Abbot Trithemius (1462–1516) who advised novices to 'procure of a lapidary a good, clear pellucid crystal of the bigness of a small orange'. That was the easy bit. They then had to 'Get a small plate of fine gold to encompass the crystal around one half; let this be fitted on an ivory or ebony pedestal.'

Paracelsus, the Swiss alchemist, in the early sixteenth century stressed the necessity for 'ten parts of pure gold, ten of silver, five of copper, two of tin, two of lead, one of iron filings and five of mercury'.

Today's scryers, or crystal gazers, are more practical. The old-fashioned glass floats used by deep-sea fishermen, for example, are said to be more than adequate for the art of crystallomancy. They are to be found in coastal junk shops and are usually hollow, transparent or green.

Whatever the globe is made of, there are some solemn rituals to be observed.

It must be kept clean. Some practitioners recommend a cleansing solution of water and brandy; others, rinsing under running water. But washing in warm soapy water is tolerated.

The crystal ball may be held in the left palm of the person receiving a reading, while the seer gazes into it. No one else must touch the crystal during a reading.

At other times, only the seer may touch the ball otherwise it absorbs negative influences and becomes unintelligible.

If the energy of the ball appears to be on the wane, it should be exposed to the waxing moon for three consecutive nights concluding on the night of the full moon.

Romanies maintain that scrying instruments respond to moonlight and should be concealed from the sun. The moon is said to govern quartz crystal. Among Romanies the crystal ball is a sacred object. As such, the merely curious are discouraged from handling it.

Some Romany clairvoyants have become legends. One of them, Urania Boswell, announced in 1897 that 'Queen Victoria would see the leaves fall four times before she went to her long rest'. She also declared that 'The King who comes after her will die long before my turn comes.'

Both of Urania's predictions came true.

Like all the Romanies of her generation, Urania lacked formal schooling. But she was still able to predict the coming of radio, when people would 'sit by their own firesides and listen to voices and music a thousand miles away, same as if it was in the room'.

It was Urania, telling fortunes at Henley Regatta in 1911, who pressed Cornelius Vanderbilt not to sail on the *Titanic*. The American magnate scoffed at her warning and perished with 1502 others when the ill-fated liner struck an iceberg the following April.

Uncannily, Urania even anticipated the weather on the day of her own death. One Saturday in 1933, she announced: 'On the third day from now I shall die and on that day it will rain.'

She was absolutely right as usual.

Urania, one of the most famous women in England, died a rich woman. When they buried her at Farnborough in Kent, she was found to have left at least £15,000, a remarkable sum at the time. Relatives said she habitually stored £500 in cash in her wagon.

At the time of Urania's death her money was divided between relatives. For the majority of gypsies, their caravan was their most treasured possession. This, according to Romany custom, was burned to ashes when the occupant died.

More than half a century later, a garden in Brighton, Sussex, was the setting for a singular bonfire.

The fire was lit at six o'clock on a July evening in 1989. An old Romany woman, Eva Petulengro, had died that afternoon. Her possessions were being torched in keeping with an old Romany custom rarely seen in Britain since the turn of the century. The mourners, led by her daughter and namesake the clairvoyant Eva Petulengro, charged their glasses with brandy as they burned the old woman's furniture, shoes and clothes. Scenes like this used to be commonplace among the Romany population in England.

When Mrs Caroline Penfold died at Crediton in Devon in 1926, the 'living wagon in which she died together with all her personal belongings that could be burned, were reduced to ashes. All her crockery was smashed and buried, along with her jewellery, with the exception of one heavy gold ring which was also buried.'

Romanies are most particular in their funeral observances. Months after her mother's death, Eva Petulengro had yet to shed a tear: there is a belief among some Romanies that 'Tears disturb the repose of the dead.'

Some families fast and thorn bushes are often planted on

Romany graves. This custom survives from the days when wayfarers were buried where they fell, which was often at the roadside or on a common.

Until quite recently it was not unusual for Romany men and women to be buried with objects thought to be useful on their journey to the next world. In the case of a man called Louis Boswell, who died in 1839, these included his watch, his pocket knife, his walking stick, his silver tankard and his fiddle. Louis also departed with some gold coins.

If anyone has discovered the secret of taking it with them, we may be sure it is the resourceful Romanies!

In this world they are the most inspired tellers of fortunes. Just as no race on earth, with the possible exception of the Jews, has wandered so far, so no race has done more to spread belief in divination.

At the very least, they are artful readers of character. The author Brian Vesey-Fitzgerald was a good friend of the Romanies but a quizzical one. In his book, *Gypsies of Britain* (1944), he remarked that 'It must be remembered that deceit and imposture alone could never have been built up and supported a practice that has withstood the passage of centuries and the constant attacks of progress. There must also be some truth.'

Spells

Magic transcends both time and space. For the Romanies it is regarded as a normal and natural part of daily life. Their motto is: 'Think lucky and you'll be lucky.'

The Romany philosophy is that depression attracts depression like a vibration. To ward it off play happy music or mix with happy people. Alternatively to rise above your problem walk to a hilltop. Looking down, roads, cars, houses and people appear in better perspective.

Trees emit energy. To strengthen yourself by receiving healing energy, stand barefoot, close to the trunk of a healthy tree. An oak tree, which symbolizes strength, is a good tree to choose. In winter, hug a tree instead: if you listen, you will hear its slow, solid heartbeat.

Every morning say: 'A miracle is going to happen today.' This attracts good fortune. Within a short space of time, you will receive a brilliant telephone call, a letter or will meet someone out of the blue who will change your life for the better.

Saying: 'A miracle is going to happen today' has a magnetic and a cumulative effect. The time it takes for something extraordinarily fortunate to happen varies according to whether you are at a low or high ebb. Each time you say the words, you tune into higher forces and attract a miracle closer to you. Whatever you say is sent into the ether: a subtle fluid above the clouds, which permeates space.

Magic can work in your sleep. When you sleep, your spirit soars to the astral plane but remains attached to your body by a silver cord. Astral projection is a nightly occurrence in healthy people. Nourishment from the spirit world is fed through the silver cord to your body while you sleep. Worry prevents your spirit from leaving your body, and cuts you off from spiritual sustenance.

If you feel ill, before sleeping say: 'I want to be healed while I sleep.' Spirit will heal you overnight and you will wake feeling better than usual. By following advice given in sleep many people have miraculously recovered. This form of divination is called iatromancy.

In the morning you may remember a dream which will contain a message to let you know that you have been treated. It may feature a surgical gown, or a visit to a hospital, a doctor, a surgeon or a hilltop.

If you are unable to sleep, try praying. Most Romanies practise a form of Christianity combined with traces of 'The Old Religion' which reveres nature and nature spirits. As their survival depended upon nature, they lived as part of it.

Many former Romanies were wealthy people, and some still are. Their belief is that possessions should only be procured in harmony with what is right and good. Simplified, good is creative and evil destructive.

To them, the gypsy *vardo* or caravan was mainly a place to sleep. Much of their work, living and cooking was carried on outside where they were in touch with the elements. They believe that the body is a vehicle for the spirit on earth, rather as the *vardo* is a vehicle for the body on earth.

There is a mystical affection between Romanies and the moon, which is permanently linked with the earth and a constant companion on our journey round the sun.

The ancient horns symbol for the moon is connected to agriculture and fertility on the earth. The emblem is likened to the horns of an ox, used for sowing. It is also associated with horseshoes, which have been in existence since the Iron Age. Oxen, as well as horses, were once shod.

Because the moon turns the tide and our bodies are mainly composed of water, we wax and wane with the moon. Generally, psychic energy is highest when the moon is waxing (becoming full) and weakest when it is waning (diminishing in size).

The moon influences the rhythms of life. When casting spells to attract someone or something into your life, you will tune into the natural flow by working when the moon is waxing from new to full. The new moon is dark for three days before it appears as a crescent. New moon spells are best worked when the crescent can be seen.

For banishing spells, to remove negativity and bad situations, you should work with the waning moon from full to new.

By aligning your energies in this way, and tapping into the natural life tides and currents, you will increase the effectiveness and power of your spells. But the most important ingredient of any spell is love. Thought and prayer are very powerful. What makes the magic work is your thought and faith.

Some spells are fuelled by candle flame, which has its origin in fire worship. Romanies guard their fire carefully in case the elements of wind and rain put it out. It feeds and warms them and, in the past, kept beasts at bay. A fire can be a purifying agent or a destroying demon. It is also used to 'torch a *vardo*': set alight the Romany caravan after the occupant's death, so that removal of their earthly possessions frees them to travel the spirit world.

The trees, herbs, flowers and oils used in the spells blend in with nature's forces. Some are governed by certain planets, forming a specific link from heaven to earth. Harmonizing with their subtle vibration awakens an echo and brings results. Any spell you cast should come from the heart, with feeling. Direct your thought like an arrow towards a target.

Do not be disillusioned if you feel that your spell has failed to work: it may only be your impatience which makes you doubt. Doubt is inverted faith, and nature cannot be rushed. Spells work in spirits' time. What is sent out mentally leaves an etheric trace, which adds power to the spell when repeated or reworded.

Faith in a spell intensifies the imagination and supports what is willed. Both words and thoughts are a powerful vibratory force. You must believe that what you wish for will come true.

Love

---

your heart's desire

You have met someone you desire. According to the Romanies this spell will ensure they respond.

Find out when the sun rises. You will need a fresh rose. At bedtime, visualize the face of the person you desire.

Place a red candle on each side of the rose. Sleep.

At sunrise, go outside or sit by an open window facing east with the rose in front of you.

Inhale the perfume and say aloud: 'This red rose is for true love. True love come to me.'

Now light the candles indoors and imagine love burning in the heart of the one you long for.

Keep the candles alight day and night until the rose fades. If they are extinguished the incantation will be broken. When the rose is dead, pinch out the candles. Bury the rose.

to win the heart of the one you love

Write the name of the one you love on the base of an onion bulb. Plant it in earth in a new pot.

Place the pot on a windowsill, preferably facing the direction in which your sweetheart lives: north, south, east or west.

Over the bulb, repeat the name of the one you desire morning and night until the bulb takes root, begins to shoot and finally blooms.

Say daily:

'May its roots grow,
May its leaves grow,
May its flowers grow
And as it does so
[name of person's] love grow.'

love charm

Rosemary is a herb which symbolizes remembrance. At one time it was planted on graves and carried in wedding bouquets. It is ruled by the sun and according to the Romanies it is representative of people born under the Zodiac sign, Aries.

A heart-shaped love charm is said to inspire response from the person the maker has in mind. Such a love charm would be particularly likely to win the heart of someone whose birth sign is Aries.

In April or May, when it is in flower, pick pliable, willowy stems of rosemary and bind them together into the shape of a heart. Picture a mental image of the one you wish for. Secure the rosemary heart with yellow cotton or ribbon. If you have any threads from your partner's clothes or strands of hair, weave these in to create a stronger vibrational link. If your desired one is born under Aries, weave in a few strands of wool too.

Place the rosemary heart in a white envelope. Sleep with it under your pillow, saying before you sleep:

'Divine Love bless my sleep
My true lover I shall keep.'

The rosemary will dry with time and the life force in it fade. When you feel your spell has brought the one you want closer, burn it in a bonfire or fireplace, thinking of flames of passion.

to find a lover

On the day of a new moon, cut a red heart out of new red crêpe paper or card. If you have a wild rose, use a fallen petal which is heart shaped.

Take a clean sheet of white paper and with a pen no one else has used, write on it this incantation:

'As this red heart glows in candlelight,
I draw you lover, closer to me this night.'

Then bathe and change into night attire.

Light a red candle and read the spell aloud. Hold the heart in front of the flame and let the candlelight shine upon it.

With wax from the candle, seal the heart and spell in an unused envelope. Conceal it undisturbed for one cycle of the moon, which is twenty-eight days from the day you began your spell.

By the time the moon is new, there should be new love in your life.

to attract the one you love

On a Friday evening, light a white night-light and place it in a lantern.

Imagine that the flame is a bright flame of love burning within your lover's heart, and that the lantern is your lover's torso.

As you stare into the flame, your own passion will make the flame rise if you will it to. When it does, pour your emotions into the flame. Think positively of your lover and draw him or her into the warmth of the candle flame as it rises and diminishes.

Say:

'May this flame of passion burn within your heart
From me, you will not part.'

Leave the candle to burn itself out. Repeat the spell on consecutive nights until you receive the communication from your lover that you desire.

to strengthen attraction (1)

You love someone, but you sense they are not as keen on you. You would like them to show more interest.

To attract their affection you need a few strands of their hair and a rose-scented incense cone or stick.

Light the incense and repeat the name of the one you long for several times, saying that you wish them to love you.

Hold their hair on the burning cone or incense until it frizzles away. As the hair burns, think of their indifference disappearing and being replaced by red-hot passion for *you*!

Leave the cone or incense to burn out.

to strengthen attraction (2)

The one you desire is playing it cool while your passion is red hot. Don't despair. Work a spell! First get a packet of seeds and a pot of earth in which to grow them.

Then find a copper object that appeals to you. On a night when the moon is waxing go outside and hold the copper object in the moonlight.

Repeat the name of the one you desire thirteen times. Each time you say this, turn the object over in your hands, thirteen times.

The Romanies say that copper attracts love and that the magnetism of the moon will draw your sweetheart to you.

Bury the copper in the earth in the pot, and carefully sprinkle the seeds on top to form the initial of your flame's name.

Love will start shooting your way like Cupid's arrows and will grow as the seeds germinate. So keep the seeds watered and the pot in warmth and light.

to get a lover to call

This spell is appropriate if you have had a lovers' tiff and you want your partner to make the first move towards a reconciliation. Out of the blue, they will telephone, write or reappear. But you need a photo of them.

The spell is best begun when the moon is waxing, but if you cannot wait that long, begin weaving your spell regardless.

Take a photo of your lover and a photo of yourself. Using a paper-clip or something similar position the photos face to face so that both faces are literally on top of each other. The idea is that the person you want to contact you cannot see beyond your face.

Place the photos in the bottom of your underwear drawer and leave them there. The person you want should respond very quickly.

According to the Romanies, crossed spoons and two spoons in a saucer are said to augur a wedding!

to entice love

This spell can be used to draw a lover closer or to attract love into a life devoid of a partner. It should be worked on the night of a new moon.

Take a salt and pepper pot or a pair of ornaments. One is to represent the female, and the other the male.

Using a piece of pink ribbon, tie the female object to one end and the male to the other, leaving about a 300 millimetre length of ribbon between them.

Every morning, untie the knot at either end and move the objects a little closer together before knotting it again.

Eventually the salt and pepper pot or objects will touch. Leave them bound together for seven days before you untie them. By this time, love should have entered your life or your existing partner should have drawn closer.

to bind a lover to you

You need a pack of Tarot cards. Separate the Major Arcana. These are twenty-two cards which number 0 to 21.

From the Major Arcana extract the card which represents the astrological birth sign of the one you wish to bind to you. Also remove the card that represents your own Zodiac sign. If you share the same sign, you will need to make a photocopy of the card.

ARIES: 21 March–20 April – The Emperor IV
TAURUS: 21 April–20 May – The Hierophant V
GEMINI: 21 May–21 June – The Lovers VI
CANCER: 22 June–23 July – The Chariot VII
LEO: 24 July–23 August – Strength XI
VIRGO: 24 August–23 September – The Hermit IX
LIBRA: 24 September–22 October – Justice VIII
SCORPIO: 23 October–22 November – Death XIII
SAGITTARIUS: 23 Nov.–22 Dec. – Temperance XIV
CAPRICORN: 23 December–20 January – The Devil XV
AQUARIUS: 21 January–19 February – The Star XVII
PISCES: 20 February–20 March – The Moon XVIII

Simply take a hair from your lover's head, perhaps from his or her comb, and a hair of your own. Knot the hairs together with three knots. Place the strands between the two cards positioned face to face.

The Romanies use a gypsy peg, but you could use a paper-clip to secure the cards together.

Keep the cards in your purse, handbag or briefcase, or wherever you are in frequent contact with them.

When you feel the spell has worked, return the cards to the pack and burn the hair.

to enhance a relationship

Make two cloth dolls, or poppets, embracing an apple and each other. Place them on your dressing table with a pink candle engraved with the names of the people the poppets represent.

Light the candle and leave it to burn until it extinguishes itself. Remove the apple and tie the dolls together with a red ribbon for passion and a pink ribbon for love. Bury the dolls underneath an apple tree, because the apple is ruled by the planet Venus. Alternatively, place them in a drawer where they will remain undisturbed.

If you can, give the partner you wish to respond the apple to eat.

to keep a lover

Make two rag dolls filled with rose petals and sweet-scented oils including rose and apple, which are both governed by Venus.

Stitch photo faces of you and your lover on the dolls. Tie them together with red ribbon and pray they will stay together.

Wrap them in an item of your clothing and your lover's clothing then place the dolls in a drawer or somewhere undisturbed.

for reciprocal love

You have met someone and would like your love to be reciprocated.

On Friday, because it is governed by Venus, light one pink, one blue and one gold candle. Place a horseshoe and a key on either side of the candles. The horseshoe and key can be those used for cake decorations.

The key represents the key to your heart, and the horseshoe luck in love.

Take two roses which represent the pair of you. Wrap the roses, the key and horseshoe in an item of clothing which belongs to your lover. If you do not possess one, use a silk scarf which you have worn.

Place them in a bedroom drawer and leave them undisturbed for fourteen days. It is a very promising sign if the roses appear fairly fresh when you remove them from the scarf. The petals should then be placed in a pot-pourri, or the roses buried. The horseshoe and key can be kept for luck.

holding on to your love

Take some modelling clay or Plasticine. Make images of yourself and your partner. Push a few strands of your hair into the head of the doll which represents you, then press strands of your lover's hair into the head of the doll which represents your lover.

Arrange the dolls in an embracing position. Roll the dolls together into one and begin again, making new images, one of yourself and one of your partner.

Now you will be part of your lover and your lover will be part of you.

Put the dolls in an embracing position. Wrap them in a new handkerchief tied with pink cord or ribbon. Hide in a secret place where the handkerchief and its sacred contents may remain undisturbed.

This way, the Romanies believe, you will be eternally bound.

lover return

To invoke a lover to return all you need is a box of new pins, an onion and the desire for their love. If your thoughts are vindictive, you will suffer.

Begin on a Friday night by placing one pin into the onion. Imagine as you do so that you are putting a thought into your lover's mind. Say, as you pierce the onion with the pin:

'It is not this onion I wish to stick,
But your mind and heart I wish to prick.
You'll think of me night and day,
Until with words you arrive and say,
I Love You.'

Leave the onion in sunlight, to invoke enlightenment.

This spell must be repeated for seven consecutive nights, preferably at the same time each evening. When you have an onion with seven pins in it, your spell is completed. With love's blessing, plant the onion in the open.

happy families

This is for those who treasure a joyous family life with children above all else.

To ensure that the family stays together, buy enough crocus bulbs to represent each member of the family.

Fill the family's most used teapot with soil.

Now plant the crocus bulbs in the teapot so that they form an unbroken circle. As you do so, concentrate your loving thoughts on each member of the family in turn.

Place the teapot where it can be seen by the family, but out of the reach and touch of curious outsiders.

As the bulbs shoot, the roots of your family will entwine, and become closely bound. As the crocuses grow and bloom, so will your family life flourish.

The spell grows in strength as the bulbs mature.

to conceive a baby

Women's menstrual periods can be likened to the moon's twenty-eight-day cycle.

Buy a hollow, cardboard Easter egg which divides into two. The Romanies use an empty duck-egg shell, or the shell of a free-range chicken egg. Whichever you use, you also need a doll small enough to fit into the egg.

On the night of the new moon open the egg, place the doll inside and leave it on your bedroom windowsill. Close the egg the following morning.

Repeat every evening for twenty-eight days. When ovulation begins, wrap the doll in a scarf and place it in a drawer where it will remain undisturbed.

When ovulation ends, repeat the process. According to the Romanies, it should not be long before you conceive.

and baby makes three

Take some Plasticine or modelling clay and make images of yourself and your partner. Blend them into one.

Now form the Plasticine into new images of yourself and your partner and of the baby you yearn for.

Link the three pairs of hands. Place the models in a new handkerchief and tie with green cord or ribbon.

Bury the handkerchief in a pot or window-box or in the garden.

Now make love two nights before a full moon, on the eve of the full moon and on the night of the full moon.

The Romanies say your wish is sure to be fulfilled.

---

to conceive a son

At your most fertile time of the month, place one red rose in a vase on a table. Light a red candle. This is symbolic of Mars, ruler of vigour and vitality.

Next, light a green candle. This colour is associated with Venus, love and harmony. Place it to the right of the red candle.

A third candle, yellow, to represent the sun, should be placed above the red and green, forming a triangle.

Three is a powerful number because it represents the male reproductive organs, and therefore sexual force.

On a bay leaf, because bay is ruled by the sun, write: 'I wish to conceive a son.' Place it face up between the candles.

Now close your eyes and imagine a red rosebud in your womb. Visualize the rosebud unfolding and coming into bloom.

Open your eyes and visualize the candlelight being channelled into your womb, then close your eyes and continue with the visualization for as long as you can.

Leave the candles to burn themselves out. Take the bay leaf, kiss it three times and place it under your pillow where it should be kept for the duration of your fertile phase.

All that is now required to complete the spell is your partner.

to conceive a daughter

You need to prepare and work this spell when you are reaching your most fertile time of the month.

Take some Plasticine and mould it into a figure representing how you might look as a pregnant woman. Cut out a photo of your face and place it on the doll's face. Press hair from your brush or comb into the doll's head and shape it to resemble your own hairstyle.

Dress the doll, or poppet, in the style of clothes you wear. The idea is to make the doll resemble you as closely as you can.

When your poppet is prepared, place her on a bed of fresh lavender or on a pink scarf sprinkled with lavender oil. Take her to a table, and to the right of her light a pink candle in a room without electric lights switched on.

Using clean, white paper write your wish: 'I wish to conceive a daughter.' Place the paper beneath the lavender or scarf. Lavender attracts love. It is ruled by Mercury and its element is air.

Fold the paper around the doll on her bed and tie a yellow ribbon or cord around her.

Place your doll beside your pillow, or in a drawer close to your bed-head, with a piece of quartz crystal and a moonstone. Quartz is sometimes called 'sacred fire' because it intensifies the rays and energy of the sun, a masculine force. Moonstone, governed by the moon, is a feminine, emotional stone. Its nature and aura improve health and reveal the future. Like females, it changes with the moon: it transmits energy to health when the Moon is waxing and gives power to desires when the moon is waning.

Lavender is a masculine flower, as its shape dictates. The desire of your partner completes the spell to bring it to fruition.

reconciliations

You have fallen out with a close friend. The fault was theirs. You want them to accept this and let bygones be bygones.

Choose a hyacinth bulb. Take a new pin with a blue top. Insert it into the bulb and imagine you are planting the thought that your friend should get in touch. The thought you sow will take root in your friend's mind.

Bury the bulb in a pot, window-box or in the garden. As the bulb grows and eventually blooms, so your friend's thoughts will turn increasingly and favourably to you, until they feel compelled to return.

Happy days await.

_____

now it's over

It was terrific while it lasted but the flame of love has sadly burned out.

If only your ex-love would accept this. They will if you write their name on a new piece of white paper.

As you do so, imagine a life in which you welcome each other as friends only.

Now fold the paper as many times as you can, seal it in a new envelope and hide it in the corner of a drawer where it cannot be disturbed.

Once you are certain the spell has worked, be sure to burn the paper. You will now be left in peace.

love divinations

To divine the initial of a future partner's Christian or surname, here is a Romany saying that they made after they
adopted Christianity.

Take an apple and peel it without allowing the peel to
break. Holding the peel in your right hand say:

'Saint Simon and Saint Jude,
On you I intrude,
With this paring, to discover,
The first letter of my own true lover.'

Turn around three times anticlockwise before throwing
the peel over your left shoulder. It is said to fall in the
shape of your future lover's initial.

Another custom is to hang the peel inside a door. The
first person who enters will bear the same initial as your
future partner.

love divination

Take an apple pip and give it the name of your lover.

Place it in a fire. If it pops, the person loves you. If it burns silently, true love is said to be absent.

To see whether a couple will marry, place two pips together in the hollow of the fire. If both pips shoot off in the same direction, a marriage will take place.

If the pips go in different directions, so will the couple concerned.

If both pips burn in silence, the Romanies say, a marriage proposal will never be heard.

lover come back

Your lover's attention has been wandering. But the situation is not hopeless.

Wait until Friday, because Friday is governed by the Goddess Venus.

With your favourite pen and fresh white paper write your first name and your lover's surname. Draw a square round them.

With your eyes closed say aloud: 'Our fate is sealed. We are one.'

Cut the square out and place it inside your pillowcase or among your most intimate possessions. Your lover will return.

_____

to get loving response

Your partner's attention appears to be waning. They don't telephone when they promise to and don't appear to be making much effort to please you.

Take a photo of your partner and a quartz or glass crystal ball. If you do not possess one, use a magnifying glass.

Place the crystal over their face and you will see that it magnifies the features: the eyes and mouth appear to move and come to life.

Tell the person in the photo what it is you want them to do.

According to the Romanies, he or she will get the message and respond.

superstitious love

According to Romany folklore it is unlucky to present a married couple with a gift of a knife. It symbolizes that their love will be cut in two.

Scissors and any other cutting implements bode misfortune. However, the recipient can counteract the impending doom by giving a coin to the person presenting the sharp object.

It is unlucky to find a knife. The finder should not pick it up.

To drop a knife is a sign that a man will visit; to drop a spoon, a woman; and a fork, a fool.

To find a length of red ribbon, red lace, red cord or red wool is an omen of luck in love. The finder should pick it up and while doing so, make a wish regarding the one they love. If they have no one special in mind, it signifies that a new love will soon be making a dramatic appearance. Either way, it should be kept as a love amulet.

One marriage custom that continues to be observed is the belief that it is unlucky to marry in Lent: 'Marry in Lent and you will live to repent.'

During a marriage ceremony, for the bridegroom to look over his shoulder to the aisle as his bride approaches is most unfortunate. The Romanies say, it symbolizes that he will always look behind him in regret.

to rid yourself of an unwanted lover

Friday is the recommended day to work this spell.

Light a new blue candle, blue being a healing colour.

Ring a little bell three times.

On a clean white piece of paper draw a circle to represent the sun and a crescent moon, with the curved shape to the left, to represent the waning moon.

Stain the paper by squeezing on to it the juice from an apple. Fold the paper in half, then a quarter. Fold what you hold into half and a quarter again, imagining as you do so that you are folding up and containing the love you once shared.

Burn the paper in your candle flame and place the ashes on a clean white saucer. Dip your forefinger in the ashes and write the initial of your former lover on your forehead. Divide the ashes into seven equal parts and evenly sprinkle them into seven pieces of clean, white paper.

Fold the seven pieces of paper containing the ashes into seven little envelope shapes. Avoid spilling the ashes because by doing so you will disperse the essence of the spell.

Pour a little candle wax over the seal of each parcel. It is most important to think loving thoughts about your partner as you do so.

Bury each parcel with love in your garden.

According to Romany folklore, if the surname of a couple who plan to marry begins with the same initial, it does not bode well. They say: 'If you change the name but not the letter, you marry for worse and not for better.'

Another belief is that the first of a couple to fall asleep on the honeymoon night will be the first to die.

to rid yourself of a persistent and unwanted lover

For this spell you need an item of your former lover's clothing.

From the material, cut a square large enough to write his or her name on.

On the night of a full moon light a pink candle. Write your former admirer's name on the cloth. Chalk works particularly well.

Wishing your suitor well, burn the name on the material in the candle flame, while saying: 'This light will burn out any flames of passion [name of person] has for me. He (or she) is gone, I am free.'

Leave the candle to burn down until it extinguishes itself.

To conclude the spell, the candle stub should be burned or buried in the remains of the clothing from which you cut the square.

---

a little love folklore

Romany folklore says that you will be rich in love and wealth if you marry at the time of a full moon. A couple can expect better prosperity by marrying when the moon is waxing than when it is waning.

Monday for wealth,
Tuesday for health,
Wednesday the best day of all,
Thursday for losses,
Friday for crosses,
And Saturday, no luck at all.

A Romany custom for a man to win the heart of a girl is to hang her shoe over his bed, after filling it with the bitter-smelling leaves of the evergreen shrub, rue.

A lucky omen for love is to find a natural knot in the tendrils or shoots of a willow tree. Willow is governed by the moon. The Romanies believe the knots are tied by fairies. To un-knot one would undo your luck.

These knots are regarded as precious love amulets. Such is their magic potency that one placed under the pillow of the person you desire is said to bind you for ever.

to mend a broken heart

Take a couple of bay leaves, a bottle and a cup to a stream, river or spring.

Sit quietly, cry if you wish and imagine your pain ebbing away downstream.

When you are composed, fill your cup with water and a bay leaf or two. Loosen your clothes and sprinkle a few drops of the potion on your heart. Then say aloud:

'This water of life will chase the sorrow from my
   heart,
This herb will soothe my pain.
I am happy again.'

Toss the bay leaves into the running water. Fill the bottle with water and take it home. Place some fresh bay leaves and water in the cup next to your bed. Leave it for three nights. By the third morning your heartache will have vanished.

_____

the eternal triangle

You are undecided between two admirers. It is vital that you make the right choice. Magic can help.

Take two tulip bulbs. With a new pin scratch the name of each suitor, one on one bulb, one on the other.

Remembering which bulb represents which lover, plant the bulbs beside each other in a pot, window-box or in the garden.

The bulb which blooms first will reveal the admirer who is most deserving of you.

vanishing spell

This spell can be used if your partner is having an adulterous affair. It is also effective in ridding yourself or another of a bad partner.

You will need a photo of him and her. If you have a photo of the couple together, separate them by cutting them apart with a pair of scissors.

Make two Plasticine dolls to represent the couple.

Cut around the photo figures and place the photo of him on the male doll and the photo of her on the female doll. Put the doll of the woman in the sea for protection. Bury the doll of the man in the earth so that he cannot see her.

This spell gets rid of the man. But if it is a woman you wish to remove, place the doll of the man in the sea, and the doll of the woman in the earth.

There should be no bad thoughts when you carry out this procedure. Bad thoughts will rebound sevenfold on you, the sender.

Romany love formulas

Essential oils can be used in spells to generate a higher vibration. The following concoctions are used for anointing candles and for blessing objects such as poppets and Plasticine dolls. The formulas are not designed to be worn on the skin or used in bath water.

In anointing a candle, drops of oil should be rubbed towards the top of the candle, which is regarded as the North Pole, and from the centre towards the bottom, which is regarded as the South Pole.

It is believed that the vibrations of the person anointing the candle are transferred to the candle, making a spell more personal and more potent.

romance magnet oil

2 drops ylang ylang oil
2 drops sandalwood oil
2 drops clary sage oil

To attract love, Romance Magnet Oil is rubbed on to a pink candle which is then burned for three hours a day. The candle should be snuffed rather than blown out, the reason being that a spirit resides in the flame and to blow it out would blow your prayer or wish away. In an existing relationship, the ritual may be ended when harmony is established or resumed.

To attract a lover, a pink candle dressed with Romance Magnet Oil should be burned for three hours a day, every day until the person fixed on makes an advance. If you have no one special in mind, burn the candle until a potential lover appears.

lover's oil

5 drops rosewood oil
5 drops rosemary oil
3 drops tangerine oil
3 drops lemon oil

Lover's Oil may be used to create a harmonious vibration to enhance a relationship. A candle can be consecrated with Lover's Oil and lit half an hour before you have arranged for your date to arrive.

marriage oil

2 drops frankincense oil
3 drops cypress oil
2 drops sandalwood oil

Marriage Oil is used to reinforce a marriage relationship, whether the union is good or floundering. It may also be applied to steer a relationship into the culmination of marriage.

Simply burn a pink or lilac-coloured candle sanctified with Marriage Oil when you and your partner are together.

desire oil

3 drops lavender oil
3 drops orange oil
1 drop lemon oil

Desire Oil is said to entice another to desire you. Possibly they already do, but they need a little encouragement.

A red, orange, pink, blue or white candle should be anointed. It should be lit when you and your partner are together.

If you love someone and they are showing no response, light a candle blessed with Desire Oil. Speak their names when you light it and allow it to burn for two hours before you snuff it out. Repeat the procedure every day until they react in favour of your wish.

to avert divorce

Divorce is taboo among the Romanies: they aim to marry and stay married.

A spell to heal a broken marriage and to reunite a couple involves little more than an apple, true love and the sheer determination to keep the marriage intact.

The advantage of this spell is that a link has already been established. The marriage simply needs reinforcement or bridging.

Buy a perfect-looking apple. If it is summer or autumn, pluck an apple yourself. An apple you pick has more life force in it than one you purchase. If by coincidence you are given an apple, the message is that you are being given a second or one last chance to heal a rift. Use it to take control.

Cut the apple in half. Regard it as an auspicious omen if the pips have not been severed with the knife, but don't fret if they have.

On a piece of clean, unused white paper write her full Christian and marital surname. Next to it, write his.

Cut around the names so that they will fit between the apple halves. Place the names on paper between the two halves and imagine the marriage being healed.

Skewer the apple halves together with two pins placed diagonally from right to left and from left to right.

When you position the pins send your love to your partner and ask for the love to be reciprocated.

Romanies use their campfire to bake the apple. You could place your apple in your hearth or in the oven to bake until the apple appears whole.

If you can get your partner to eat some of the cooked apple, so much the better.

Love

Romanies never burn ivy on a fire, because it is an ever-green; woodland spirits are said to take refuge in evergreens in winter when the other trees are bare.

nether garment spell for fidelity

Although Romany marriages endure and divorce is taboo, it does not mean their marriages are necessarily more happy than most, or that partners do not go astray. But there is a spell which draws a partner home to their original ties.

It is very basic, as down to earth as the Romanies themselves. It gets to the point and apparently works.

Choose a pair of your partner's pants and a pair of your own. Take two nutmegs. Write your partner's Christian and surname on one and your own Christian and marital name on the other.

Bind the two nutmegs with a red cord to symbolize passion. Wrap them in the underwear. Place them in a clean white envelope. Sleep with them under your pillow if your partner is away, or embed them in a drawer where you keep your favourite or most sensual clothes.

when a son or daughter leaves home

When your grown-up son or daughter is leaving home, this spell will help to protect them. Apart from lots of your love, you need rose pot-pourri or fresh roses or rose oil. Roses are governed by Venus, the planet of love.

To form a psychic link, make a poppet – a little doll to resemble your child. If knitting is something you do around your offspring, you should knit one; if you sew, make a rag doll. If you do neither, use Plasticine.

Whichever type you make, use belongings of your child such as their hair or clothes. Inside the doll, place some of your child's hair in the area of the heart. Give the doll your son or daughter's hairstyle and dress sense.

In a dark room, light a pink candle for love and place the doll in front of it. Sprinkle the poppet with pot-pourri or oil, or place the roses in his or her arms.

Send your love to a son or daughter who may have left against your wishes, implore them to visit, write or phone to let you know their telephone number, address or point of contact. The Romanies say the poppet will ensure they respond.

While you let the candle burn down and extinguish itself, take the doll to your child's bed and leave it comfortably tucked up until your offspring returns. If you are using pot-pourri in your spell, wrap the doll in a scarf to keep the rose petals around the poppet.

For a young child, perhaps coming home from boarding-school, to find a doll looking like them in bed might be frightening, so make sure you have removed the doll before your son or daughter sees it.

Place it in a drawer of your own until you put it to bed again to represent your beloved child in their absence.

joint custody

Although Romanies themselves try to avoid divorce, they can advise friends who have lost a partner and who may want to fight for the custody of their children. This is the way they go about it.

Take The Lovers VI from a Tarot deck along with The Sun XIX. The Sun represents two children, a girl and a boy, and the love you and your partner once shared to conceive them.

But your family may consist of more than a girl and a boy.

If you have one son, choose the Ace of Wands.
If you have two boys, select the Two of Wands.
If you have three boys, remove the Three of Wands, and so on.

Daughters are represented by the Cups suit.

If you have one daughter, remove the Ace of Cups from the deck.
If you have two daughters, select the Two of Cups.
If you have three daughters, pick the Three of Cups, and so on.

Place the sons and daughters cards in a row according to their birth sequence.

Light a pink candle to represent each daughter and a blue candle to represent each son.

Place the child cards on either side of The Lovers VI card.

Put a photo of the family on the left of the candles, and one to the right of the candles.

Position a blue candle above the photos and a blue candle beneath the pictures.

'These pictures are in motion,
Love is the potion,
These children are my emotion.'

Write the children's names on a piece of paper and burn them in the flame: blue for boys and pink for girls.

Take objects such as teddy bears and dolls which represent each child and place them in front of the candles in an embracing position.

Pray for your children to love you, but most of all send your love out to them.

Leave the candles to burn down. Meanwhile take the cuddly toys which represent the children to your own bed, or the beds the children sleep in.

Bless each toy and each bed. Go to sleep and believe in the power of the spell.

unwanted divorce

When an unwanted divorce appears likely, the Romanies advise a friend who wants their partner to return to light a purple candle. Pierce it with a pin from right to left, so that the pin tip appears through the left side of the candle.

Take a pin with a blue knob and pierce the candle from left to right. The point of the pin should be mentally focused on crossing the symbolic path of the other person in their tracks. Leave the candle to burn and extinguish itself. Afterwards, bury the pins.

Go to a river, with a shoe belonging to the missing partner. Write your wish upon it. Toss the shoe downstream. The couple's problem will ebb away.

If the friends' divorce is an amicable one the Romanies may advise them to light a yellow candle in an otherwise darkened room.

to communicate with an absent partner

Take a photo of your partner and look into their eyes. You can look deeper into their eyes and beyond, into their mind, by placing a crystal ball, a magnifying glass or a glass-based ashtray on a photo of their face.

Speak directly to the photo or through the object you have chosen to magnify the features of the face. The eyes, mouth and facial features will move in such a way that it appears you are speaking directly, face to face. At this point you have made communication.

Tell them what it is you want, or ask a question and they will answer telepathically. Their verbal response will enter your mind.

Blow out the candle and wave the photo through its smoke from north to south and west to east. Return the photo to where you normally keep it.

to mend a cracked marriage

Crack a walnut and remove both halves from their shell.

Take an acorn to represent him and a conker to represent her.

Take them into the garden or have a pot of earth at hand. In an easterly position, symbolic of change and new beginnings, bury each walnut half, placing an acorn on one and a conker on the other.

Romany love and marriage customs

If a courting Romany presented his neck-scarf to his girl-friend, and she constantly wore it, it was a sign that she loved him. Such a gesture might incite him to propose.

Among the Welsh gypsies, 'jumping the broomstick' used to be a marriage ceremony. The broom was a branch of yellow, flowering gorse cut from a heath or woodland. If broom, which flowers in spring and summer, was out of season, birch or heather, both associated with fertility, were used instead.

Locks of hair, cut from the heads of the couple getting married, were plaited by the bride. She concluded the plait with a lovers' knot which is similar in shape to the figure eight, formed twice. The ring symbolized a never-ending knot of love, which would survive death, a perfect wedding ring. A gold ring would be bought and worn after the honeymoon. Rings made from rushes instead of hair were sometimes used.

A wedding breakfast fire would also be built with broom or birch for the congregation to sing and dance around while musical instruments were played. The wedding toast was drunk in home-made wine or cider.

The early household sweeping broom was made from broom, birch twigs or heather. It was customary for the gypsy woman whose husband had made the broom to present it to the bride. It symbolized not so much a life of servitude as sweeping the negativity out of married life. Meanwhile, other menfolk would prepare a bower, a little alcove, beneath a birch tree, where the couple, when married, could make love. Gypsy women added the finery.

For love, luck, health and prosperity, the Romanies

believed in breaking bread over the heads of the bride and groom.

The bread was made by mixing flour with fresh or dried fruits combined with a little blood taken from the ring finger of the couple.

Today's tradition of throwing confetti and watching the bride and groom cutting the wedding cake at a traditional white wedding, is a remnant of the ritual which English peasants practised, and which the Romanies adopted.

When Olive Rawlings, the last Romany girl in Britain to be born in a horse-drawn caravan, fell in love with non-gypsy, Dave Cox, he had to comply with centuries-old courtship rites and family tradition.

Before Ilene and Dave Rawlings consented to their daughter's parish church blessing in front of a congregation of forty in Berwick St John, Wiltshire in 1982, Dave had to travel with Olive's family for a year, to prove whether or not he could adjust and earn a living. His tests included carving pegs from hazel wood, and being able to build, drive and repair a wagon and care for and ride a horse bareback.

Luckily, Dave proved a worthy husband and he and Olive went on to have two children, and brought them up as proper Romanies in their horse-drawn caravan.

Health

The Romanies' word for uncleanliness is *mockadi*, which sounds similar to the slang word 'muckety'. The nature of their life and fight for survival has made them extremely fastidious. They always possess a series of stainless steel bowls, each one kept for a particular function and that function only.

One bowl is used to wash vegetables, a second one for meat and another for food utensils. A fourth bowl or series of them is used for carrying out their own ablutions. An individual bowl is used for washing clothes, and a further bowl for tablecloths, tea towels and dishcloths. It would be extremely *mockadi* to wash anything in the wrong bowl. Cracked and chipped china is discarded. Animals are designated their own plates or bowls, which are washed in further separate bowls. An animal is never permitted to lick a plate from which a Romany eats.

The independent Romanies, after hundreds of years of wandering, had to be their own doctors. They learned how to use herbs, plants and other remedies to cure them when they were sick or injured.

They strongly believe that many illnesses begin in the mind. Thinking you are healthy can actually make you fit. A Romany mother who says to a son or daughter who has bumped their head or cut their finger, 'Let me kiss it better', gives the child faith to feel fitter. Whether someone at a distance is aware of it or not, the Romanies also say that sending love to a sick person improves that individual's condition.

You can help speed someone's recovery by lighting a blue candle. With as much imagination as you can muster, visualize your sick companion encircled by blue light. Imagine the sun shining upon them and warming their body, illuminating their life and making them well again.

Leave the candle to burn out. Repeat daily if your friend is very ill. The effects will multiply.

---

depression

Romanies always try to look on the bright side of any situation. That way, a problem is more likely to turn out well. However, if that is not so easy, try this Romany antidote to the blues.

Peel several cloves of a garlic bulb and place them in a saucer. Pour white vinegar over the cloves so that they are partly immersed in it.

Place it beside your bed while you sleep. The garlic is said to be turned pink by the negative energy it absorbs.

The cloves should be buried in the morning and replaced by fresh cloves at night.

to give up smoking, nail biting or any other habit

Nine strands of hair belonging to the person who has the habit should be wound around an iron nail. The nail should then be hammered into a wooden post. The obsession is believed to decline as the nail rusts. Another remedy is to think every night, before dropping off to sleep, that you will abandon a habit or addiction. (See p. 26.)

To grow a good head of hair, Romanies say:

'Of weak thinning hair you will never complain,
If you cut your hair in the moon's wax
And never in her wane.'

Hair removed from a brush or comb should be buried or burned. It is believed that if a magpie builds a nest with it, the person from whose head it has come will meet an untimely death. The magpie is regarded as a bird of ill omen because its feathers are the same colour as a clergy-man's robes.

The curse of ill luck that a single magpie flying from right to left is said to bring may be neutralized by saying: 'Good morning Mr Magpie, how's your wife?' If it is after midday, to avert misfortune you can say as you bow: 'Good day, Your Lordship.'

predicting the sex of a baby

To determine whether a baby expected will be a girl or a boy requires a location where red and white roses grow together.

The pregnant woman, with her eyes closed, should be guided to the rose bushes. She should then walk seven times in an anticlockwise circle before heading, still with her eyes shut, towards the roses.

If the rose she picks is white, a daughter is predicted; if red, a son.

A more well known method is to dowse with a pendulum. A ring suspended from a length of cotton or a human hair can be used instead.

The pendulum, as it is held over the mother's tummy, should be asked to swing in a clockwise circle if the baby is a boy and in an anticlockwise circle if it is a girl.

to remove warts and verrucas

To remove a wart or verruca rub it with a stone then place the stone in a tissue or handkerchief.

Give the stone in the handkerchief to a friend to bury at a crossroads. The wart will wither as the handkerchief containing the stone decays.

Instead of stones, dried beans can be wrapped in tissue, each one representing a wart or verruca. The parcel should be tossed over your left shoulder, at a crossroads.

Another method is to rub the wart or verruca with a potato instead of a stone. No handkerchief is required. As the potato disintegrates when buried, so will the wart.

Someone's wart can be bought for a penny. The person selling the wart should place the coin between two halves of a potato, which you bury for them.

An alternative to remove several warts or verrucas is to rub them with a piece of chalk. Using the same piece of chalk, a cross should be drawn on the trunk of an ash tree while reciting the following rhyme:

'Ashen tree, ashen tree,
Pray take these warts from me.'

A further chalk method involves rubbing each wart or verruca with a piece of chalk and then drawing a cross on the back of a fireplace. The warts are said to disappear gradually as soot covers the chalk marks.

Or to charm warts and verrucas away, you can tie as many knots in a piece of string as there are warts. The warts will decay with the string if the string is buried.

Alternatively take a pin. Point it at the wart or verruca without touching it and tell the wart or verruca that it will be gone. Stick the pin in turf or soil. The wart or verruca withers as the pin rusts.

The insides of either a broad bean pod or a banana skin rubbed on warts and verrucas can also make them disappear.

sympathetic sorcery to ease ill health

According to the Romanies, there is no simpler way to cleanse someone of an illness than to cut the fingernails and trim the hair of the person who is sick.

The hair and nail clippings should then be buried. Others say they should be thrown into a stream, river or running water, which will wash the illness away.

to alleviate illness

Take a coin you have found on the ground and put a pinch
of salt on it. Place the salt in a small amount of boiling
water to dissolve. When the water has cooled, use the coin
to flick the saline solution on to the palms of the hands and
soles of the feet of the patient.

Another remedy to alleviate illness is by candle magic.

Using a pin and a blue candle, inscribe, from the base to
the tip, the name of the person who is ill. Pierce the candle
with a pin and leave the pin in position.

Let the candle burn down and extinguish itself. The pin
will remain intact and should be kept for future spells.

to lower a fever

A salt spell to lower a fever involves throwing a handful of salt into the flames of a fire. Salt turns the flames blue. Look into these blue flames, and visualize the patient well again while saying: 'Fever burn, good health return.'

to ease lingering ill health

This spell was traditionally used by mothers for their children.

Go to a stream, hold an empty jar in the water and let the current fill the jar. Take it home. Place seven cloves of garlic in the water and seven pieces of coal. Leave it to steep for seven days. Meanwhile, find a three-forked twig.

Boil the contents of the jar and stir it with the twig. When cooled, flick the water seven times on the patient. This is believed to avert the 'evil eye', a spirit of misfortune.

It is also thought that illness can be washed away by going to a stream on a new or full moon to rinse the sick person's hands and face in the water.

---

protection

This protection spell can be used to improve the health of an elderly person as well as to keep harm away from someone who is fairly housebound.

Take a horseshoe or an iron nail. Bless it by immersing it in salty water. Bury it in the garden of the sick person or in a pot plant with the tip poking out of the earth, to act as a conductor to disperse the energy.

Say when you bury it:

'Ill health I do tell,
Run through this iron
[name of person] is free and well.'

to increase health and vitality

A quartz crystal vibrates a frequency of energy. Romanies who use a crystal ball for clairvoyance often ask their clients to hold the ball and to make a wish on it (see pp. 19–21).

Sometimes they use quartz rock crystal to heal.

If you have a piece of quartz, wash it in warm soapy water and rinse it with running water.

Hold the crystal in both hands. Close your eyes and imagine being bathed in white light. Visualize the area of your illness and point the crystal to your illness site. Imagine a stream of light flowing from the crystal and bathing the area in its pure rays.

Place your crystal under your pillow while you sleep.

to remove a headache

To remove a headache, rub your forehead with a stone and then embed the stone in earth. The ache is said to be absorbed by the soil.

Alternatively, rub a headache away by rubbing a horse-shoe on your forehead. A piece of iron is said to work just as well.

A further method is to lie down and place a quartz crystal on your pillow. If lying down is inappropriate, quartz held to your head for a few minutes is said to relieve the symptom.

If a Romany has a bleeding nose, some drops of blood are allowed to fall on the earth. They are then covered with soil for earth spirits to work their healing.

to help heal broken limbs

Pick up twenty stones when you are out for a walk. These represent ten fingers and toes. If an arm or a leg is broken choose a long-shaped stone to represent the limb.

Wash the stones under running water to remove any dirt. Place them in a bowl of water with silver-coloured coins. Sprinkle in some salt. Light a blue candle and say:

'With this salt I consecrate these stones
And heal the broken bones.'

Remove the stone which represents the broken bone and wrap it in a comfrey leaf, tying it with a blue ribbon or thread. Carry as an amulet and bury when the limb has healed.

to ease cramp

The Romanies say that sleeping with a bowl of stream or spring water under the bed relieves cramp.

Another remedy is to place in the foot of the bed corks which have been threaded along red cord, or wrapped in a red silk scarf.

for sight and insight

To improve eyesight and clairvoyant vision, boil a little spring water with a pinch of saffron on a Sunday. Astrologically, saffron is ruled by the sun and dedicated to magic and love because of its colour. Being one of the earliest spring flowers, it reveals light after darkness. Romanies say it instantly soothes painful eyes if they are bathed with it, and that it also increases clairvoyant vision.

Another method to relieve sore eyes is to put gold rings in the ears. Perhaps this is why so many Romany children as well as adults have pierced ears.

bad breath

The Romany remedy is to eat at least one fresh, raw apple every night, before going to bed. Another antidote is to chew parsley, peppermint, fennel or caraway seeds.

A branch of apple blossom indoors is said to be a forerunner of ill health. Neither should may blossom be brought into a home because its red and white colours are said to symbolize blood and bandages. But a wish for health made on may blossom, which is governed by Mars, will come true.

Blossom steeped in water helps to remove splinters.

The saying: 'Ne'er cast a clout till May is out', regarding taking off clothes due to a warmer weather change, refers to may blossom on the hawthorn bush and not to the month.

Romanies never point at a rainbow. Doing so is said to invite illness. But it is believed that a wish made facing a rainbow in the open air will come true.

bump on the head

To alleviate swelling when a child bumps its head, the blade of a broad-bladed knife is pressed against the bump. The knife is then thrust seven times into the earth so that the pain may be transferred from the child to the ground.

To stir food or drink with a knife is 'to stir strife'.

A Romany remedy for healing a cut is to place jam mould on the gash. The penicillin in the mould is said to help heal the laceration.

sneezing

'Coughs and sneezes spread diseases' – and according to the Romanies, sneezing is more than a sign of a cold.

Sneeze on a Monday you'll escape a danger,
Sneeze on a Tuesday a kiss from a stranger.
Sneeze on a Wednesday a good news letter,
Sneeze on a Thursday a gift which is better.
Sneeze on a Friday news will cause sorrow,
Sneeze on a Saturday you'll travel tomorrow.
Sneeze on a Sunday ask God to bless you
All the week, your health to keep.

whooping cough

The Romany remedy is to go to a beach when the tide is turning and to get the person with whooping cough to drink sea water until they vomit into the sea. The cough is said to be washed out with the tide.

These days, because of pollution, it is undoubtedly better to induce sickness in some other way!

baldness

A Romany remedy said to make hair grow on a balding patch is to mix equal measures of rosemary oil, almond oil and bay rum and to rub that into the scalp morning and night.

Garlic oil rubbed into the scalp morning and night is also said to make hair grow where there are signs of it thinning.

An infusion of half a teaspoon of rosemary sprigs in 250 millilitres of water, used as a warm rinse is thought to strengthen hair and prevent loss.

dieting

You want to lose weight, but you have a sweet tooth and cannot resist cakes, biscuits or chocolate. This spell will make it so easy to abstain from eating them that you will be amazed.

Take a piece of cake, a biscuit or a chunk of chocolate and bury it in a pot or in the garden.

For each of the foods you wish to stop eating, plant three cloves of garlic on top. The garlic will purge you of your craving, which will have disappeared completely by the time the garlic has grown.

drug taking

The Romanies have their own way of getting someone off drugs. You will need several metres of yellow ribbon and if possible, but not necessarily, the name of the drug supplier.

Place twenty-one night-lights in a circle surrounding a photo of the drug taker. Twenty-one candles are used because three times seven is a very magical number.

Yellow ribbon represents sunshine and is a link from mother to child. Tribes used to hang the umbilical cord of a newborn baby on a tree. When the child grew up, they would talk to the tree to protect the person it belonged to while they were in danger or hunting.

While the candles are burning, take the ribbon and tie bows on to branches of an elder tree. Elder is believed to prolong life and deter evil spirits. As you tie the bows, imagine you are binding your child with protection and filling their life with sunshine, health and happiness.

If you know the drug dealer's name, write it on a piece of paper and bury it at the root of the tree, asking for the roots to absorb the dealer's bad influence.

When the candles have extinguished themselves, remove the photo.

to recuperate from illness

Hold a glass of spring water in moonlight, so that the water catches the light. Drink the water, simply asking the moon to take the illness away to the next cloud it disappears behind, and also with its wane.

absent healing

To heal someone at a distance, you need a feather, rosemary oil, a shell, a stone and an onion.

Write the name of the person you wish to heal on the onion (a ballpoint pen or pencil works well).

Plant the onion bulb in a pot or in the garden, placing a stone to the north, three drops of rosemary oil to the south, a shell to the west and a feather to the east. Cover the objects with soil.

Place the pot on a horseshoe, or place a horseshoe close to the bulb if it is in the garden. Both the onion and the horse are governed by Mars, the God of War. This spell uses the strength of Mars to win the battle over the illness.

Pets

---

to heal a cat wound

To heal a cat after a scrap, the Romanies recommend that you should light a blue candle. Place your cat on your lap or let the cat find its own comfortable place to lie. Soothe it with loving strokes until it purrs or appears relaxed and comfortable enough to stay put for five or ten minutes.

Close your eyes and pray for a spirit vet to work through your hands. After a few minutes you should feel heat emanating from your palms. You may then feel your hands being guided to various parts of your cat's body. Direct them to where they are drawn.

Imagine the colours of the rainbow – red, orange, yellow, green, blue, indigo, violet – streaming into the cat.

Finish by thanking the spirit vet who used your hands to channel healing energy. Then say: 'Kitten scrap scrabble scrap' before giving your cat a kiss to seal the spell.

Cats have been revered as magical since the time of the ancient Egyptians. A cat washing itself is believed to be a forecast of rain. To see it wash behind its ears is a sign that a visitor will call. If it sits with its back to the fire, it is a sure sign of frost.

Your cat may also assist divination. Leave a door open and think of a question which can be answered yes or no. Call your cat into the room and notice which is the first paw it places on the floor. If it is the right forepaw, yes is the answer. If it is the left, the answer is no.

dog healing

The Romanies strongly believe in the power of hands-on healing for dogs, horses, and smaller pets including rabbits, guinea pigs, hamsters, mice and birds.

It is not an alternative to visiting a vet. But it may be used in conjunction with veterinary treatment, before or after surgery, or simply if your pet appears to be 'under the weather'.

Place your dog in a comfortable position or let it find its own spot in which to lie down.

Sit beside your dog and pray for a circle of gold light to be placed around you both for protection, and for a circle of blue light to be placed around you and your dog for healing. Then say the Lord's Prayer.

Place your hands palms down over your pet.

Visualize yellow light, then blue, green, indigo and violet rays permeating through your hands into your pet's body.

End by asking for a cloak of spiritual protection to be placed around your pet to protect and keep it from harm.

This can be repeated several times a day.

---

horse whispering

Horse whispering is shrouded in mystery. It is an inexplicable method employed by the Romanies to tame wild and temperamental horses.

Tradition says the 'horse whispering' secret was granted as a deathbed legacy from a horse charmer to his eldest son. The Romanies say that one who has received the gift of horse whispering cannot die peacefully until they have passed on the talent.

There are tales of horse whisperers meeting secretively in moonlight to practise their equestrian skills and to discuss hypnotic, herbal and magical formulas.

Some believe horse charming is the application of herbs or aniseed to the horse's nose or bridle or the recitation of the Lord's Prayer in its right ear. Whatever it is, it is a secret the Romanies guard jealously.

One spell which is said to make the horse fearless of traffic and supernatural beings is to draw a circle on the left front hoof with a piece of coal and a cross on the right front hoof. The horse is then given a piece of salted bread to eat which the charmer has spat on seven times.

horse protection spell

Place the horse where it can see the campfire. In front of it dig a small hole and throw into the hole some hairs from its mane and tail. Trace the left front hoof on the ground. Then dig out the earth inside the hoof shape and sprinkle it by hand into the hole to bury the horsehair.

This form of sympathetic magic is said to prevent the horse from being stolen or becoming ill.

A fertility rite to encourage a mare to produce foals is to feed her oats from a gourd. Its shape represents a womb. If gourds are out of season, a woman's apron is said to serve the same purpose.

---

psychic dogs

Leaving dogs tied outside caravans cannot be condoned. One reason why gypsies do this is because dogs are considered *mockadi* (dirty): they wash their own rears, whereas horses do not.

The Romanies say that dogs, cats and horses are psychically receptive to their owners' thoughts.

When your dog is beside you, if you mentally tell it that you are going to take it for a walk, it will get up to go.

Another method is to stand in a different room to your dog and tell it you are going to take it for a walk, or are going to feed it. Again, see if it will respond.

pet at the vet

When your pet is away at a cattery, the kennels or at the vet's, to strengthen the psychic link with it and ensure its safe and happy return, place a blue ribbon or cord in a circle around its bed, or favourite chair and toys. Tie a knot to form a circle. Only unknot the cord when your pet is back in your safe keeping.

Wealth

money spell

Around campfires or in their sunny *vardos* the Romanies invoked spells to bring riches, or at least a comfortable living. The following spell has been popular for centuries; in the past, coins of an earlier date were used, preferably gold.

Take five short green candles and ten 50-pence coins. Rinse the coins in warm salt water. Set five saucers in a circle and place one coin in the centre of each saucer.

With a little melted wax, securely fix a lighted candle on top of each coin. Distribute the five remaining coins inside the circle so that they form a five-pointed star with the apex facing away from you.

Say aloud: 'I need X amount of money immediately.'

Imagine green and purple five-pointed starlight glowing from the candle flames. Imagine coins cascading from the flames for several minutes. Let the candles burn out naturally. Provided your need is genuine, a windfall should be on its way.

When it arrives, say thank you to the mystic world.

Tarot money spell

The Romanies strongly believe in Tarot cards (see p. 18). This spell to receive money takes fourteen days to perform, fourteen green candles and the Coins suit, which totals fourteen cards, taken from a pack of Tarot cards.

On the night of a new moon, light a green candle. Take the Ace of Coins card from a Tarot deck and place it face up, flat on its back, behind the candle.

Sit for a few minutes looking at the candle flame, thinking about what you will do with the money you wish for. Leave the card in position and allow the candle to burn down and extinguish itself.

On the following evening, light a new candle. Place the Two of Coins card, face up, to the right of the Ace of Coins and slightly below it, to begin forming a clockwise circle of cards. Sit gazing at the flame and ponder again how you will use the money you want. Leave the card in place and the candle to extinguish itself.

On the following night perform the same sequence, using a new candle and the Three of Coins card. On the fourth evening use the Four of Coins and continue until on the tenth night you have placed the Ten of Coins card in position and left the candle to burn down.

On the eleventh night, use the Knave of Coins card. The picture on the card depicts a young man giving you money. Dwell on the thought as you look into the flame.

On the twelfth night, place the Knight of Coins card in position and allow your imagination to wander regarding what the picture on the card suggests.

On the thirteenth night, use the Queen of Coins card. Again, allow your imagination to drift as you look at the card and candle flame. The Queen depicts a woman giving you money.

On the fourteenth night, which will be a full moon, your last card will be the King of Coins. He has money in his hand and is giving it to you.

Leave the cards in position and let the candle burn out of its own accord.

The following morning, return the suit of Coins to the pack. Money should start rolling in!

wealthy week

On a Sunday evening, burn a gold candle surrounded by heaps of loose change. It is important not to count the cash. If there are so few coins you cannot help but notice, cover them with a handkerchief. Watching the candle flame, say: 'Thank you for the money I have already received from the invisible world.'

Leave the candle to burn down and extinguish itself. Afterwards gather up the coins. You will need them for the next evening's spell.

On Monday burn a white candle in the same way, adding to the heap of coins any more you have accumulated throughout the day. Repeat words of thanks for money already received from the invisible world.

On Tuesday use a pink candle and add to the coin collection the loose change the day has brought you. Speak the magic words again.

Continue with the words and the same coins, adding daily to the pile. Use a red candle on Wednesday, a green candle on Thursday, a blue candle on Friday, and on Saturday a green candle.

Stash away your cash and reserve it for money spells. The more coins you accumulate, the greater the power of attraction.

Alternatively, throw the coins into your purse.

---

urgent money spell

The Romanies say that when money is urgently needed by a certain date, this spell works wonders. Because it is a spell where help comes metaphorically, a minute before midnight strikes, it must be performed at the witching hour of midnight.

Take one night-light to represent each £100 or £1000 that you critically need. Stand them on a plate you often eat from.

At a quarter to midnight, sit in a room with no electric lights. Light a gold or silver, green or white candle separate from those representing money. This is the candle which will give power to the 'money' night-lights and will enable you to see what you are doing.

Now work your magic. Pray for a circle of gold light to be placed around you for protection and for a circle of blue light to be placed around you for healing.

Pick up a night-light and light it from the main candle flame. As you do so, say that the night-light you are lighting represents the £100, or £1000, you need. Place it on the plate to begin a circle of 'money' night-lights.

Light each night-light, and say the same words for each until the circle is complete.

Say a prayer explaining that you are not being greedy: that the money is necessary.

Leave the candles to burn out of their own accord. The money should start winging its way to you.

A saying associated with dropping money is: 'Money on the floor, money to the door.'

Tradition says that if you drop money and someone else

picks it up for you and puts it in your hand, it is an omen of more money to come.

It is unlucky for the recipient of a gift of a purse or wallet not to receive a coin inside it.

oiling the wheel of fortune

The following ancient Romany formulas can be used to enhance the vibration of your spells. They are designed for anointing candles, coins, paper or other objects mentioned in this book. They should not be worn on the skin.

money-drawing oil

3 drops wood marjoram oil
2 drops lemon oil
2 drops eucalyptus oil

Romanies roll their notes, rather than keep them flat. Smearing the outside note with Money-Drawing Oil is believed to attract a cash increase.

lucky planet oil

5 drops ylang ylang oil
3 drops clary sage oil
5 drops geranium oil

Lucky Planet Oil rubbed on an orange candle, which is then left to burn down, is said to encourage a lucky turn of events.

commanding oil

6 drops patchouli oil
8 drops myrrh oil
16 drops sandalwood oil

Commanding Oil is dabbed on uncounted coins, which are

then placed in the light of a full moon as a statement that money is required.

_____

compelling oil

> 8 drops sandalwood oil
> 4 drops myrrh oil
> 2 drops cinnamon oil

Compelling Oil is known to have been used to encourage business deals along. Sometimes it is smeared on a candle which is lit the night before a negotiation. Alternatively it is used to anoint money used in a transaction to ensure future business with the same person.

_____

lady luck oil

> 4 drops sandalwood oil
> 7 drops rose oil
> 5 drops lavender oil

Romany women are said to anoint their clothing with Lady Luck Oil, to ensure success when hawking or fortune-telling. It is also used on candles and money.

_____

power oil

> 5 drops frankincense oil
> 2 drops cypress oil
> 3 drops juniper oil

Power Oil is generally used to strengthen any spell, whether it is for health, wealth, love or happiness. A few dabs on clothing helps a person win in a situation where they feel the odds are stacked against them.

money attraction

Light a green candle. Let it burn for five minutes. Blow it out, rub your hands in the smoke and imagine money coming to you.

Another simple spell to attract money requires a new moon and a shiny new coin. On the night of the new moon, place a coin on a windowsill with the head facing up. When the moon is full, to encourage money problems to diminish, turn the coin so that the tails side is facing up.

Keep the sequence in harmony with the phases of the moon or finish the spell by removing the coin on a new or full moon.

Bubbles floating on a cup of tea augur money. A floating twig or rectangular leaf denotes a letter or phone call – from a man if dark, from a woman if light.

When the moon is new, you can open the channels for money to come spiralling your way by using a spiral money spell.

Collect as many coins as you can muster. Light a green candle and place it on the left of a table. Now work only by the candlelight.

To the right of the candle, form the coins into a spiral shape until you have exhausted your change.

On clean white paper, in green ink, write the amount of money that you need, and the reason. At the end of your wish add 'By the grace of God'. The reason for this is that it is important that the money should come through good fortune.

Place the wish to the right of the coins and leave it there

until the candles have burned down. Scoop up the coins to spend or keep.

Put the paper containing the wish in your wallet or purse, where it should be kept until your wish has been fulfilled.

to increase wealth

When the moon is new, secretly place a £10, £20 or £50 note underneath the front doormat inside your home. It will be charged with positive energy every time a visitor or family member walks over it.

The greater the value of the note used, the larger your returns are said to be.

The note should only be removed when the moon is full, otherwise you will attract unexpected expense to your door.

Another way to attract money into your home is to plant marigolds on top of a golden-coloured object.

Whether they are in a pot, tub, window-box or your garden, the marigolds should be as close to your front door as possible. They are ruled by the sun and commonly flower all summer long. Because there are so many varieties it is possible to have marigolds in flower every month of the year. This is why they are also known as calendula.

On the night of a new moon, and in moonlight, place as many notes and coins as you can muster on a windowsill.

Avoid the temptation to count the money because that limits the boundaries of expectation. The greater the amount of money, the greater you can expect your financial increase to be.

Say: 'Oh beautiful moon, please radiate wealth into my life with your light.'

Your financial fortune will begin to flow and show signs of fruition at the full moon. To keep money flowing, repeat the spell when you next see the crescent of the new moon appear in the sky.

*   *   *

Friday is sometimes referred to as 'Tip Tod's Day', meaning the Devil's day. Work should never be commenced on a Friday for the simple reason that it is unlikely to be finished.

What you give is said to return sevenfold.

Take a note of any denomination. Light a green candle. Write on green paper a wish for wealth and prosperity. Place your wish in an envelope and seal the envelope. Blow out the candle.

Now decide whether to give the money to the next charity caller who knocks at your door, whether to post it to a charity or give it to the first charity collector you see in the street.

It is important to the spell that the offering is sacrificed as soon as possible.

You will reap what you sow.

---

to win on a bet

Light seven green candles and say:

> Abracadabra
> Abracadabr
> Abracadab
> Abracada
> Abraca
> Abrac
> Abr
> Ab
> A

Repeat seven times and extinguish the candle. Do this for seven days. When you place your bet you are more likely to win.

Romany horse dealers use the term 'Lucky Penny' when making transactions. The dealer returns a coin or banknote to the buyer, for luck.

the lottery

The Romanies often like a gamble. They advise this spell for the lottery. Light six green candles. Each represents one of the six winning numbers.

Sit quietly and ponder the flames, allowing each flame in turn to suggest a number.

Fill in the form according to the numbers which come into your head. Sprinkle the sheet with nutmeg and snuff out the candles. Leave the form dusted with nutmeg for a day before thoroughly brushing it off and taking it to be fed into the computer.

job hunting

Although Romanies are historically and instinctively nomads they sometimes want to stay in one place. This means they must seek work, perhaps on a farm, or find an outlet for their trade. This is a typical job-hunting spell.

Take a bath or a shower at bedtime. Sprinkle a heaped teaspoonful of the herb valerian into a teapot. Cover with boiling water. Steep for a few minutes before drinking.

Valerian is governed by the planet Mercury, symbolic of trade and commerce, good fortune and wealth. The ancients worshipped Mercury as the God and giver of good sleep and pleasant, prophetic dreams. He guarded against nightmares and blessed sleeping children with a smile on their lips.

As you drink, imagine yourself setting out to work in the job you are after. Say aloud: 'This valerian will take me to a land where dreams come true.' Go to bed and drift into sleep.

In the dream that follows, you will be told how to obtain the job you seek. Your subconscious mind will ensure that you take the right steps to get it. Good luck or as the Romanies would say, 'Kushti bok!'

an interview divination

Take two acorns. One represents you, and the other the person you have applied to for a job.

Place both acorns in a bowl of water. If they float side by side, or touch, you will get an interview. If they float in opposite directions, you will not.

An omen of money luck is to see a spider weave its web in the morning. This announces that money will be coming in. The web must not be removed until money has arrived. It is especially fortunate if the web is on a window or door. Spiders have been revered since ancient times, and because their webs contain penicillin, they have been used by Romanies to cover cuts and wounds. Spiders must never be killed. If they spin long webs it is a sign of good weather; a short web predicts rain.

If you want to live and thrive
Let a spider run alive.

---

to get a job at an interview

Before you go to your job interview, you will need a green candle, a banknote and a paper clip.

Light the candle and show both sides of the banknote to the flame. Fasten the note to the back of a photograph of yourself. Blow out the candle.

Carry your photo, with the note attached, in your hand-bag or wallet, to your job interview.

A Romany saying to induce money luck is 'Trinka Five'.

to prevent redundancy

Romanies sometimes wanted to stay longer in one spot when an employer told them there was no more work, the equivalent of today's redundancy. They responded with this spell.

Soak the labels off seven green bottles. Green is used in this case because it represents abundance.

Place two of the empty bottles upright. In a sack or thick carrier bag placed on newspaper, smash the remaining five bottles with a hammer. Wear gloves and goggles so that you don't cut yourself or get flying glass in your eyes.

Using a funnel or one made from rolled paper, fill the bottles with the broken glass. On a piece of unused white paper write: 'I will not be made redundant from [name of employer].' Place the note in the neck of one bottle. Write the same message again, and insert it in the second bottle. Seal the tops with a cork or cap.

Dig a hole facing south to north and place the bottles so that one bottle neck faces south and the other, north.

Bury the bottles. Forget about them and losing your job. The spell ensures that all channels are free to keep work flowing your way.

The Romanies say that it is a very auspicious omen of wealth if a frog hops across your path.

---

getting justice

Occasionally, Romanies fall foul of the law, mostly concerning the siting of their caravans. Feeling innocent and wanting justice, they invoked this spell.

Take the 'Justice' card from a Tarot deck. This represents the Scales of Justice which preside over the Old Bailey in the City of London. Now light a blue candle and place the Justice card on the right-hand side. Write your name and address on an unused piece of white or green paper and place it to the left of the candle. Romanies sometimes use their thumbprint instead.

Light thirteen night-lights, to represent the 13 lunar cycles of a year, and place them in a circle around the candle and card.

Say a prayer in which you ask for protection to be placed around you and your family.

Write your wish regarding the legal matter on a piece of paper. Sprinkle it with rose oil and burn it in the blue candle flame. Place it on a saucer until it turns to ash. Leave the candles to burn out and your wish will be fulfilled.

Happiness

horseshoe wishing spell

After the Romanies arrived in Britain in the fifteenth century (see p. 12), they protected themselves with a positive attitude and were busily self-sufficient. Whatever wasn't good, wasn't worth thinking about and they were mostly content. With their constant search for happiness and talismans forecasting good luck, their culture and mysticism began to be absorbed into local folklore. Here is an early example.

Many Romanies were once blacksmiths. And today to find a horseshoe symbolizes luck. It is especially fortunate to find a shoe with nails in it. Each nail denotes a year. The more nails, the more years of luck lie ahead. Others say each nail represents a year the finder will have to wait before marrying.

A horseshoe nailed to a door, or over a door, is said to act as a protective amulet. It attracts good luck and defies evil to cross the threshold. Placed with the open ends pointing upwards, it catches good luck and keeps the luck in.

To cast a spell with a rusty horseshoe, first brush the rust off with a wire brush so that the holes are open. Light a red candle in a room with no other light. Sit in front of the candle and write seven wishes on seven small squares of paper.

Use green paper for a money wish; blue for health; pink for love; red for employment; purple or lilac for friendship; yellow for spiritual concerns; orange for legal matters; brown for the home and white for miscellaneous matters.

Make sure your wishes are precise, because fuzzy ideas get fuzzy results.

Roll the squares tightly and poke them through each hole in the horseshoe. List your wishes on a separate piece of paper, numbered from one to seven, from left to right on the shoe, so that you know, at a later date, which hole holds each specific wish. Snuff out the candle.

Place the horseshoe in a shoe or boot box and hide the box away. It is important at this point to forget your wishes. Only return to the horseshoe to remove the slips of paper and tick off on your list when any of the individual wishes come true.

stone spell

A stone with a hole through it is regarded as an amulet to ward off evil. It should be threaded on cord and hung on or over a door, to act as an all-seeing eye.

It can also be used as a wishing stone.

Wash the stone in running water to cleanse it. Write your wish, with chalk or a pen, on the stone. What you wish for is now 'written in stone'. Make sure your request is precise and leaves no room for loopholes.

When the sun is setting, embed the stone in soil facing west. Beside it place a piece of blue cord, blue cotton or blue ribbon with a knot to represent your wish. Fill the hole in the stone with allspice. Sprinkle the spell with water and speak your wish while you cover it with soil.

The winds of change will bring your wish to you. Do not doubt, or think about your wish once you have buried your stone.

to meet with success

A Commanding Spell: This spell will place you on the threshold of success. It may also be used to raise power before an important meeting.

Light a blue candle in front of a mirror. Sit at the mirror and stare into your own eyes in search of your soul.

Ask for a circle of gold light to be placed around you for protection and a circle of blue light to be placed around you for healing. Repeat your Christian name or names twenty-one times.

Then speak your wish and repeat it twenty-one times.

Blow out the candle and await success.

key to happiness

The Romanies believe that it is extremely lucky to find a key. The augury is that you will soon, metaphorically, be opening a door to success, in love, marriage or work, or perhaps getting a new car. Happiness is assured.

To find an old key is magical. It is said that the finder will experience spiritual mysteries and have prophetic dreams. They will become a channel of communication from heaven to earth.

But to break a key is an unfortunate omen: it predicts a broken relationship.

Take a key. Light a white candle. Visualize the metaphorical door you wish to open with the key. On a piece of paper, draw a door to open your wish.

Pour some candle wax on the drawing of the door and place the key in the wax, to weld the two together. Let the wax cool. Fold the paper round the key to form a neat envelope or parcel. Generously seal all the edges with more wax from the candle. Blow out the candle.

At night, go to a bonfire and toss the parcel in, imagining strongly what door it is you are passing through. Pour your passion into the flames and send it heaven bound. The spell has been cast. Do not dwell on your wish because such thoughts drag it back to earth and sap its energy. Have faith. Believe in the miracle which will happen very soon.

white heather spell

White heather has notoriously been hawked by Romanies as a good luck talisman. Ruled by Venus, it is said to be lucky to wear but unlucky to keep in the house. Indoors it is an omen of death.

A very simple spell to attract good fortune into your life is to plant a circle of seven white heathers at your front door.

The pure vibration heather exudes neutralizes malevolent forces and clears a path for good fortune to enter.

needle spell

If a needle is accidentally dropped, and found poking upwards, it foretells a visitor before the end of the day. The needle should be picked up and kept according to the saying:

Find a pin, pick it up,
And all day long you'll have good luck.

To extend your luck for longer than one day, place the needle in a vase of fresh water and fresh flowers. The essence of the flowers will energize the luck in the needle and your luck will last longer than the flowers.

When the flowers die, discard them as usual, empty the water and put the needle in your sewing kit as a reminder of your good luck.

birthday spell

It is unlucky to cry on your birthday. If you do, it is said, you'll cry all year through.

Making a wish when you blow out candles on a birthday cake is traditional, but you can also conjure up a happy year ahead with flowers.

Write your birthday wish on a piece of paper and keep it under a vase of flowers. Or plant a seed or bulb while you think of your wish. Your wish will grow with the plant.

handkerchief spell

To give someone a handkerchief is a sign that you will be parting from each other. A borrowed handkerchief should be returned.

Tying a knot in a handkerchief as a reminder to do something is similar to a Romany wishing spell where a knot is tied to represent a wish.

to pass an exam

At one time, local councils sent tutors to Romany encampments. After a lesson, the children were left with exercise books designed to teach them how to read and write. There were written questions and tests to complete before the next visit.

In their *vardos*, or beside the campfire, the family cast spells. Put a blue cloth, scarf or handkerchief on a table. Place a pile of books relating to the exam on top.

Light a yellow candle and place it facing south, beside the books. Light six white candles clockwise in a circle around the yellow candle. Make your wish, say: 'I will pass this exam. I will achieve.' Leave the candles to burn for a few minutes while you visualize sitting the exam.

Snuff out the white candles in an anticlockwise direction and finally blow out the yellow candle.

To remind you of success, you may like to carry the blue scarf or handkerchief with you to the exam. If a child is taking an exam, place a piece of quartz next to the books, and give it to them to carry as a good luck amulet on the exam day.

love of mother-in-law

Whether married or not, your partner will be happier if their mother likes you. You must win Mother-in-law's love, by sending your love to her.

Choose a Friday evening, when the moon is waxing. Take a pink candle and write your wish around it. Your wish should come from the heart. It could be: '[Mother-in-law's name], love me.'

Take a pin with a blue head, for healing, or a yellow head, for enlightenment. Between the beginning and end of your message, pierce the candle with the pin so that its tip emerges on the other side of the candle.

Light the candle and imagine the light of the flame warming Mother-in-law's heart. Leave the candle to burn down and extinguish itself, and salvage the pin.

Now have a tulip bulb ready, because tulips are said to heal rifts and reunite. Confirm your wish as you push the pin into the bulb. Then bury the bulb in a plant pot or garden. Your mother-in-law's love for you will grow with the bulb.

straying pets

When a cat, dog or other pet has gone missing do not despair. Pets are tuned in psychically to their owners and will respond to an invisible call even at a distance.

Place some food and milk or water in the pet's familiar bowls. Light a blue candle next to them and say:

'My fair beauty gone astray
Please come back to me today.
With my yearning heart and wonder,
Please come back to me from yonder.'

Afterwards, leave the candle to burn down, or snuff it out when your pet returns.

To deter a pet from straying, dig a hole and then fill it with salt, charcoal and fur from your pet's brush or comb.

Another custom said to prevent a cat or dog from straying is to cut out a piece of soil bearing the animal's footprint.

The soil should then be placed under a strong tree in your garden. Willow is preferable. Alternatively, keep the print indoors in a pot plant or dish.

A well-known means of preventing a cat or dog from leaving home, particularly after a house move, is to rub its four paws with butter.

---

missing caged pet

A bird, hamster, guinea pig or rabbit which has gone astray can be welcomed home.

Call its name three times. Tie a yellow cord around its cage, in which you have placed fresh food and bedding.

Call its name three times again.

to have an object returned

Pick a convenient time of the day or night when you will be able to sit undisturbed for five minutes.

Will the object to you, that someone has failed to return. If you sit wishing it back into your life, the thief will telepathically feel uncomfortable, until finally they bring the missing item to you.

Another method is to place an iron nail on a windowsill. It should be pointed north, south, west or east, according to the direction in which the person who has the object lives. Simply will the object back, every time you look at the nail. When the object has been returned the nail should be buried or restored to the tool kit it came from.

Another Romany retrieve remedy is to place a rose beside a similar object. Love, symbolized by the rose, will prick someone's conscience and the object will be returned.

to get another to agree

Light a pink candle for love and a blue candle for healing
on a Friday evening. Snuff them out after casting your spell.
  Say:

  'Please . . . do think again.
  May the consequence heal my pain.
  Grant my request to me and you'll see,
  The good in your heart set me free.
  Bless you.'

to remove misfortune

To extricate yourself or someone you care for from a string of ill luck and misfortune is not difficult, according to the Romanies.

Take three small jars and nine garlic cloves. Stick numerous white rose thorns into the garlic cloves and place three cloves in each jar.

Each jar should be buried within sight of a church porch while you say the Lord's Prayer.

to make friends with fate

Fate, it is said, may be influenced in your favour by knowing your personal magic word. You can remind yourself of your magical word mentally or speak it verbally, when you feel that you need a boost of energy.

Light a white candle and sit facing south. Take a dictionary. Close your eyes and turn the book round several times so that you are unaware of which way it is facing.

Eyes closed, fan a wad of pages until you feel compelled to stop at a certain page.

Eyes still closed, wander about the page using your forefinger until you feel inclined to pause. Open your eyes. Look at the word under your finger. If there is more than one, pick the first that instinctively jumps out at you from the page. This is your magic word.

Speak the word mentally whenever you wish to tune into a situation. It will change the vibration around you and attract good influences.

weather spell

No need to cross your fingers and hope for good weather. According to the Romanies, you can make the sun shine whenever you want it to.

Light a golden candle. Draw a five-inch map of the area where you want the sun to shine.

Clockwise, circle the map three times around the candle flame, imagining it is the sun.

Burn the map in the flame making your wish. It could be:

'Fair weather I ask you to shine,
On this special day of mine,
I've chased the clouds away,
So the sun will shine all day.'

Your special day will be filled with sunshine.

Another simple sunshine spell is to write the date and day on which you wish the sun to shine, on an orange candle to represent the sun.

Domestic ill luck can be avoided by never washing blankets during the waxing May moon. According to the saying: 'If you wash blankets in May, you will wash a loved one away.'

To stir up the wind to dry washing on a line, stand with your back to the breeze and exhale facing the washing. To make it less windy, inhale and blow the wind back in the direction it is blowing from.

If rain is your desire, whipping pond water with a hazel stick is believed to invoke a downpour. This is known as 'water witching'.

Happiness

Rooks remaining in their nests in the morning is believed to be a sign of rain. When a blackbird sings a very shrill unusual tune, it is a sure sign that rain will follow.

co-operation of a child

To cross your fingers and make a wish under a birch tree is said to be very lucky: the wish will come true.

The birch, governed by Venus, is believed to exude magical loving properties on parent and child relationships.

Take your child or children with you to a birch tree. Ask them to make a wish, with their eyes closed and fingers crossed, to become good children who do as their parents tell them to.

temperamental children

A spell to encourage a child to be less self-centred and more caring of parents and family, uses a narcissus bulb to represent each child and a hyacinth bulb to represent each parent. Firm-based bulbs work best. You will also need a glass bowl and pebbles in which to grow them. Some nurseries and hardware shops sell glass containers for water culture of bulbs.

In Greek mythology Narcissus was a beautiful youth who spurned the love of a nymph named Echo. He lost his heart to his own beautiful image reflected in a clear pool of water. The gods took pity on him and changed him into the flower that now bears his name.

To begin your spell the whole family could go for a country or seaside walk to pick up stones or pebbles which they feel drawn to. Enough stones are needed to partially fill the glass bowl.

Afterwards, soak and wash the pebbles until they are thoroughly free of mud or sand. Place them in a glass bowl and put the bulbs on top. Fill with water and make your wish.

Place the bowl on a window-ledge and watch your child or children's behaviour become more considerate and loving as they grow. If support is needed when the bulbs bloom, use blue ribbon or cord to send healing to your family.

to encourage sibling rivals to be friends

Pick a wheatsheaf to represent each feuding son and an oat straw to symbolize each argumentative daughter.

Soak the wheatsheaf and straw until they are pliable. Twist, plait, weave or bind them together according to how many strands you are handling. Then tie them in a knot to form a circle, symbolizing that their ties cannot be broken.

Toss it into a stream, a river or the sea and ask for the squabbles to be washed away by the current or the tide.

brotherly and sisterly love

To draw children in a family closer, as well as to stop them bickering, take water from a stream or river. Bring it to boil on a fire built with fresh twigs. Write the name of each child on a bay leaf and let them simmer together in the water. Ask Venus to bless them.

With a pin, inscribe the names of the children on a pink candle and then light the candle, so that its flame may flicker over your spell.

Take a pink, a blue and a green ribbon. Knot them together and make a plait. Knot the ends and tie a knot in the middle. The first knot represents will, the second, wisdom and the third, activity.

Remove the pot. Leave it to cool and extract the leaves. Allow the candle and the fire to burn down.

In the garden or in an unused flower pot, bury the ribbon, placing the bay leaves on top. Sprinkle ash from the fire on to the pot. Plant a rose bush or miniature rose on top. The rose is a potent ingredient in any love philtre. Since ancient times it has been regarded as a symbol of silence.

As the rose grows, the bond between the children will be strengthened. This spell is also said to work when children from two marriages are brought together.

to make a wish come true

On the day of the new moon, write your wish on a sheet of clean paper, then light a new, white night-light. At this point turn off any artificial lighting that may be switched on.

For ten minutes, enjoy the flame's glow and think about the fulfilment of your wish. Then say:

'As I sleep tonight may the divine power of spiritual love and light grant my wish.'

Concentrating on your wish, burn the piece of paper in the flame. Leave the night-light to burn out.

Repeat the spell at the same time on twelve consecutive nights. If you miss a night, begin the spell from day one.

---

divination

The herb rosemary can also be used to divine a yes or no answer to a question.

Pick a sprig of rosemary. Ask a question seven times then pluck a leaf, saying 'Yes.' Pluck another leaf and say 'No.'

Continue alternating yes and no with each leaf you pick, until the sprig is bare. The last leaf you pick reveals the answer.

The Romanies also use hair for divination.

Throw some hair into a fire. It is said to be a sign of long life if the hair flames up vigorously. It is an omen of ill health if it simply smoulders away.

To determine whether a person is flirtatious, pull a single hair from their head. The hair should then be held between the forefinger and thumb. The more it curls when released, the more flirtatious the owner.

Another belief is that if a woman's hairpin falls out, someone is thinking of her.

water divination

Romany children play at divination using water and a stone to find the answer to a question.

Holding a stone, sit in front of a bowl of water and ask a question, which can be answered with either yes or no.

Drop the stone into the water and carefully count the ripples created. An even number of ripples expresses yes; an odd number, no.

to remove a problem (1)

By practising a little cloud magic, you can easily chase away the clouds that metaphorically overshadow your happiness.

Each cloud is as unique as a human being, so choose a cloud which appeals to you. Tell the cloud that it will restore your peace of mind to see the blue sky it conceals.

Focus your mind on the cloud and imagine your problem disappearing as you mentally bore a hole through it to reveal the sky. If you can do this it is a sign that you are capable of removing any problem and that blue skies of happiness are yours.

Another method is to place your problem in a cloud. Then decide which way you want the cloud to move, to the left or to the right. Ask the cloud to move, taking your problem with it. If you gaze at the cloud for a few minutes, it will move in your chosen direction.

to remove a problem (2)

Write your problem on the sole of an old shoe. Put the shoe on, stamp on the problem three times, take the shoe off and burn it in a fire.

Another method is to write your problem on a piece of paper. Dig a hole, place the paper inside and bury it along with a piece of copper, a piece of iron and some zinc.

A simpler remedy is to write your problem on a piece of paper and to throw it into a fire.

to solve a problem

This spell is for a problem which is on your mind most of the time.

In daylight, stare into the sky for a few minutes and choose a cloud which attracts your attention.

Look at the cloud until you feel it is saying that it is ready to give you a message or to carry one for you. The message the cloud conveys may confirm a question in your mind or reveal the outcome or a solution to a problem, either telepathically or by its shape.

Alternatively, to send out a wish, look at the cloud for a few minutes without blinking. Say to the cloud: 'Please work a spell!' Then close your eyes for a few seconds, with the spell in your mind while you wish it to work.

Open your eyes, look at the cloud and place the spell in the cloud. Close your eyes for a few moments and avoid looking at the cloud again. Refrain from wondering whether your wish will come true. If you do, you will earth the spell's energy and weaken its power. Romanies say the spell usually brings a result within six weeks.

to break ill luck

Go for a walk and pick up seven twigs from the ground, one to represent each day of the week. Traditionally the twigs should be: ash for Monday; beech for Tuesday; elm for Wednesday; oak for Thursday; horse chestnut for Friday; yew for Saturday and elder for Sunday.

Take them home, snap them into pieces and burn them in the hearth or on a bonfire. Say:

'Ill luck is broken,
As these words are spoken.'

to deter an unwanted visitor

To avoid being revisited by an unwanted caller, all you need is salt. Immediately after they have made their departure, sprinkle salt, which is regarded as a purifier and a protection against evil forces, on the ground where they said goodbye.

to fulfil a wish

Write your wish on a piece of paper and burn it.

An alternative method is to write your wish or several wishes on a log or a piece of wood and to burn it in a fire. Don't think or speak about your wish once it has been consumed by flames.

To coincidentally utter the same words as someone else at precisely the same moment means that a wish will come true if the pair of you link fingers and both make a wish.

for a wish to come true

On the night of a new moon write your wish on a bay leaf. The bay tree is governed by the sun and ruled by Leo so it is particularly potent when the sun is in Leo between 24 July and 23 August. Take the bay leaf outside and look at the moon. Kiss the leaf three times and sleep with it under your pillow.

The first day of any month offers fresh hopes and new beginnings. One good luck invocation is to say 'Rabbits' before any other word on the first of the month.

Some say 'White rabbits' three times as the last spoken words on the eve of a new month. On waking they say 'Hares' three times. This is said to ensure a month which is blessed with good fortune.

Wish upon the first star seen in the night sky, on any night of the year. Your wish will come true if a second star appears shortly afterwards.

driving test

In the 1950s the Romanies' horse-drawn wagon began to decline with the widespread use of cars and motorized trailers. Whether you are taking your test for the first time or again, the Romanies say, this spell increases your chances of passing.

Take The Chariot VII card from a Tarot deck and place it between red, amber and green candles set in a triangular shape. The amber candle should be placed closest to you, the red above it, to the left, and the green to the right. The Chariot represents the car you will drive on your test and the candles, traffic lights.

Take The World XXI card and The Wheel of Fortune X card. The World represents new horizons you will explore through driving and The Wheel of Fortune, the steering wheel. Place these on either side of the green candle.

Without electrical lighting in the room, and preferably when the moon is waxing, light the candles.

Look into the flames and visualize yourself correctly answering the written test.

Pick up The World XXI card and The Wheel of Fortune X card. Imagine yourself driving to places you would like to go, alone or with a passenger. Place the cards in their original position.

Leave the candles to burn out. Take the cards with you to your written test and driving test.

home sweet home

Just as the Romanies blessed and protected their *vardos*, so you can bless your new home and protect it from burglary and fire.

Sprinkle salt around the perimeter, or plant garlic around the boundary.

Alternatively, pray for a circle of gold light for protection and a circle of blue light for healing to be placed around the home.

Disruptive neighbours who upset the harmony of your home with loud music or invasive security lights can be tamed quite simply. Place small hand mirrors on window-sills facing their home. These reflect what they are sending out to you, back to them if you say 'Return to sender.'

If no anger is attached to your actions, your neighbours will respond to your influence without realizing why they are suddenly being nice to you.

special spell dates

st valentine's day: 14 February

By tradition many species of birds begin pairing off at this time. The Romanies say that if you are unattached, a bay leaf placed under your pillow on St Valentine's Day will induce you to dream of the person you will marry.

festival of the holy marys: 25 May

St Sara of Egypt is the Romanies' patron saint. Throughout the eve of 24 May and during the 25th, gypsies exalt the elements of fire and water on which their lives depend. From wood the men have gathered, gypsy women build a healthy campfire. They cook a huge feast and gather around the fire to exchange presents and good cheer in a similar way to *gaugos* – 'house-dwellers' – on Christmas Day, which the Romanies also revere. Apart from on the Festival of the Holy Marys, gypsy men usually consider lighting the fire to be one of *their* everyday chores.

On 24 May many Romanies still make a pilgrimage to attend an annual service at the shrine of Saint Sara of Egypt, in the crypt of the church of Les Saintes Maries de la Mer in the Île de la Camargue, Bouches-du-Rhône, France. They carry the statue of St Sara, who is black, into the sea from where she originated and out again.

st swithin's day: 15 July

If rain falls on St Swithin's Day, the Romanies believe, forty days of rain will follow.

on midsummer night's eve: 20 June

To predict by dreaming who your future partner will be, before going to bed, place your shoes in a 'T' shape and say:

'Hoping this night my lover to see,
I place my shoes in the form of a T.'

for a life filled with sunshine

St John's wort, a golden flower which smells like turpentine, is regarded as an emblem of the sun.

Light an orange candle and place a bunch of St John's wort beside it. Make a wish, then hang the bunch of St John's wort over an entrance door into your home. Leave the candle to extinguish itself. It will bring you your wish and ward off evil, too.

to encourage good fortune

On Midsummer Night's Eve, take an orange, to represent the sun, and a lemon, which symbolizes the moon. Press cloves, which denote brown wooden nails, into the skin of the fruit. The cloves purge any misfortune which the first half of the year may have brought and ensure that the second half of the year will be trouble free.

to entice a lover to return

Pick five roses on Midsummer Night's Eve. Bury one under a yew tree at midnight. Place the second outside a church gate. Put the third at crossroads with the head pointing in the direction of home. Place the fourth beside running water. The fifth rose should be put under your pillow for three nights and then buried.

hallowe'en: 31 October

To find, from a list of potential suitors, whom a person is most likely to marry, take one crab apple to represent each suitor. Prick the initials of each candidate into the skin of an apple. Leave the apples in a box, undisturbed until Old Michaelmas Day (11 October). The most perfectly formed initials reveal the answer.

Another method is to take as many hazel-nuts as you have prospective partners. Name each nut accordingly before placing them evenly on the front of the fire. The nut which pops the loudest and burns most brightly says it all.

A very simple spell is to light three candles for three wishes. Leave them to extinguish themselves.

christmas

Some Romanies today make and sell holly wreaths. For the Christmas season, they rent part of a wood, to cut evergreen. The Romanies believe that a holly wreath should always include both prickly and smooth holly for domestic harmony. Prickly holly alone is an omen that the man will rule the roost in the New Year.

new year's eve

To divine whether you will marry in the New Year, throw
a shoe or boot into a willow tree, attempting to get it caught
in the branches. Willow is governed by the moon. You are
allowed to throw the shoe no more than nine times because,
in spells, nine symbolizes completion.

new year lunar spell

It is considered that a wish spoken to the new moon of the
New Year will be fulfilled. It is especially fortunate to see
the new moon crescent on your right. The first full moon
of the year is also said to make a wish come true: it will be
granted before the year is out.

The first full moon of the year is also believed to be a
mystical time when you can mysteriously see the face of
your future partner appear in a pond which reflects the
moon. This is hydromancy, divination by water, an art practised by the ancient Egyptians.

No crystal ball can be more magically charged than by
the full moon reflected in a pond. The Romanies say: 'It is
known as drawing the moon down from heaven.'

From moonlight to magic, superstition and the gift of
prophecy, we leave the Romanies by their campfire, where
if a spark flies, they will know a surprise is on its way.
There they are at one with the spirits alive in every flame,
tree, breeze and stone. And in each cloud, brook, stream
and river; in flowers, hedgerows and in every creature that
swims, crawls, flies or walks.

As a Cornish gypsy once said: 'From witches, warlocks
and worricows, ghoulies, ghosties and long-legged beasties

and things that go bump in the night, may the Good Lord preserve us.'

But Romanies by their very nature always put the fears of the night behind them. As they sit round a campfire, romance and hopes of a golden future appeal to them far more.

In the fire-glow for centuries, the elders have told the young of their age-old traditions and the spells that can bring love, health, wealth and happiness.

A flickering fire can mesmerize even the most hardened cynic. So, on a balmy summer night, when the moon is full, organize a Romany firelight party. A good bonfire would be ideal, but with a bit of imagination a spluttering barbecue would do.

In a dark corner of the garden, place a candlelit table for the local fortune-teller. Find a violinist friend to improvise the fiddling of exciting, passionate, romantic Zingari tunes. You could cheat by buying discs of gypsy music and hiding the CD player behind a bush. In the wild dancing that follows, nobody will complain.

As the fire glows and flickers, pour a glass or two of rich gypsy wine such as Hungarian Bull's Blood and you will cast a Romany spell over everyone.

As the Romanies say today: 'The Tatcho drom to be a jinneypenmengro is to dik to shoon and to rig drey zi' – The true way to be a wise man is to see, to hear and to bear in mind.